Iron Hearts and Olive Skies

-Ramesh

ISBN: 978-93-343-5794-3

First published in India in 2025

Published by Ramesh Gunasekaran

Cover Design: Ramesh Gunasekaran

Printed in India

About the Author

Ramesh Gunasekaran is a librarian by day, an English teacher by passion, and a storyteller every time inspiration strikes. Hailing from Salem, Tamil Nadu, Ramesh has a deep-rooted love for the defence sector—thanks to growing up with an ex-serviceman father and a dream of joining the Army himself (still very much in progress).

Iron Hearts and Olive Skies is his third book, following *The Chrono Voyager* and *The New Frontier: A Tale of Five Astronauts.* While he teaches grammar and catalogues books by profession, Ramesh writes stories to escape into worlds where tanks roar, friendships are forged in fire, and love sometimes hides behind a ribbon.

When he's not writing or planning library hunts for students, he's quietly wishing for a peaceful, silent life—though his characters rarely let him have one.

Title: *Iron Hearts and Olive Skies*

Contents

Table of contents

Short Introduction:

Set during the closing months of World War II, *Iron Hearts and Olive Skies* follows the life of **Stevenson**, a charming and fearless tank operator stationed with the US Army in the battle-scarred fields of Europe. At 28, Stevenson dreams not only of victory but of finding someone to share life beyond the sound of gunfire and tank engines.

His best friend **Anderson** is a walking contradiction: a lethal combat specialist with a love for terrible jokes and bad coffee. Their commander, **Rubert**, is a living legend—stoic, battle-hardened, and full of secrets from a dozen forgotten campaigns.

But war isn't just about enemies and tactics—it's about heart, loyalty, and unexpected turns. Along the way, they'll be joined by key characters: **Clara**, a courageous French resistance member who might be more than Stevenson bargained for; **Private Malley**, a fresh recruit with a poet's soul; and **Major Von Krieger**, a fearsome German officer with unfinished business.

As battles rage on, and personal missions unfold, the bond between these men will be tested not just by bullets—but by the choices they must make.

Chapter 1: The Man in the Tank

The sun wasn't supposed to shine in war zones. And yet there it was—spilling gold across the muddy fields of rural France, dusting everything it touched in a soft, lying warmth. The grass whispered beneath tank treads. Somewhere, a bird had the nerve to chirp.

Inside the M4 Sherman tank, **Private First Class Stevenson**, age 28, groaned.

"Sun's out," he muttered, squinting through the periscope. "That means some poor sniper's gonna wake up feeling cheerful."

From behind him came a voice. "You know what else is out? My patience. That was the worst breakfast I've had in my life, and I once ate squirrel stew made by a man missing three fingers."

Anderson, the team's most dangerous weapon—and worst cook—tossed his dented mess tin into the corner of the tank. "They call that eggs? Looked like someone sneezed into a sock."

Stevenson laughed despite himself. "Still better than your coffee."

"That coffee saved lives."

"It ended them, Anderson. You brewed a war crime."

Anderson grinned and patted the tank's metal wall like a loyal pet. "Ol' Betsy don't mind. She runs on hate and grease. Like Rubert."

They both froze a little at the name. **Commander Rubert** had a way of entering rooms—or tanks—when least expected. Like an armored ghost with a cigar. But not today.

Rubert was outside, staring at a crumpled map and barking orders to the radio operator like the fate of the war depended on it. Maybe it did. He wasn't the kind of man you questioned, and if you did, you better hope your boots were made for sprinting.

"Do you think he ever smiles?" Anderson whispered.

Stevenson adjusted a knob. "Once. In 1942. It caused a landslide in the Alps."

Anderson cracked a grin. "Tell me again why you joined the Army."

"To see the world," Stevenson said, deadpan.

"And?"

"I've seen mud. Explosions. French cows. One tried to sit on the tank last week."

Anderson nodded seriously. "I saw that. It had strong opinions about warfare."

They were part of the 3rd Armored Division, and this corner of France—somewhere between Saint-Lô and wherever the Germans weren't supposed to be—was now home. Their mission was simple: roll east, secure the roads, punch through resistance, and somehow not die doing it.

For Stevenson, it had become routine. Drive. Shoot. Dodge shells. Patch the tank. Eat bad food. Sleep like the dead. And somewhere in that routine, he carried one absurdly stubborn hope:

That after the war, he would get married.

Not just to anyone. A real woman. Brave, smart, able to survive a world like this. Someone who could make him laugh, or make him forget everything he'd seen. Someone who liked tanks—at least a little.

"Still thinkin' about your dream girl?" Anderson asked, noticing the far-off look in his friend's eyes.

Stevenson didn't deny it. "Yep."

"She doesn't exist, pal."

"She might."

"She's either fictional or French."

"What's wrong with French?"

"Nothing. Except I tried flirting with one and she slapped me with a baguette."

"You deserved that," Stevenson said with a grin.

"Maybe," Anderson replied proudly. "But I got a kiss on the cheek after."

A knock on the tank's hull snapped them out of their banter.

Rubert.

He swung the hatch open like he was tearing the sky apart.

"Move out in five," he growled. "We've got German armor three miles east, trying to flank the supply convoy. We cut them off at the orchard. Minimal resistance—unless they lie."

"Copy that, sir," Stevenson said.

Rubert peered at them both with those steel-gray eyes. "Stay sharp. Stay alive. And Anderson... if you tell another joke about breakfast, I'll reassign you to kitchen duty."

"I've been trying to get that job for months!" Anderson called out cheerfully as Rubert disappeared.

Stevenson flipped switches, pressed pedals, and the tank growled to life like a waking dragon. Betsy wasn't pretty, but she was sturdy. Like the rest of the team.

They rolled out with two other tanks, heading east down a dirt path half-covered in blown trees and craters. French farmhouses loomed in the distance, some roofless, some already ghosts. The scent of churned earth mixed with oil and smoke.

Anderson manned the turret, his head poking out like a curious turtle.

"Do you think we'll survive this week?" he asked.

"If we don't," Stevenson replied, "at least you won't have to eat breakfast again."

They reached the orchard by noon.

It should've been peaceful. Rows of apple trees, leaves fluttering in the summer breeze, half the fruit still clinging to branches.

But peace is often just a silence waiting to break.

A shell screamed past and slammed into the ground fifteen feet ahead.

"Ambush!" Rubert's voice crackled through the radio. "Three enemy tanks. Flank left!"

Betsy jolted into action. Stevenson swung her left, dust flying as treads chewed up grass. Anderson's hands danced over the gun controls.

"Target spotted—Panzer IV, 11 o'clock!"

"Fire!"

The cannon roared. The recoil shook the whole tank. Smoke, then fire. One German tank ignited like dry leaves in a furnace.

"Direct hit!" Anderson cheered.

But another tank responded. The shell missed by inches, knocking Stevenson against the controls. Sparks showered from a panel.

"Betsy's anderson," Stevenson muttered. "Let's make them pay for that."

Anderson loaded again. Another shot. Another explosion. The orchard lit up like fireworks on the Fourth of July, if fireworks could kill.

When the dust settled, Rubert's voice came through again.

"Good work, boys. Convoy's safe. Return to camp."

Stevenson exhaled. "Another day."

Anderson gave a mock sigh. "And not a single eligible woman in sight."

Back at camp, Stevenson sat under the stars that night, sipping coffee that tasted like burnt shoes.

Anderson joined him, eyes skyward. "You ever think about life after this?"

“Every day.”

“What if we don’t make it?”

“Then we won’t have to eat your breakfast again.”

Anderson chuckled. “Fair.”

Silence stretched.

Then Stevenson added quietly, “I still believe she’s out there.”

Anderson looked over. “Then we better survive. She won’t date a ghost.”

Chapter 2: The Woman with the Ribbon

The next morning brought fog thick as soup and quiet too strange for comfort.

Camp was silent. Too silent.

Stevenson sat beside the tank, cleaning mud from his boots and waiting for the next round of chaos. The engine of Betsy, their old Sherman, ticked softly as it cooled. In the distance, a rooster crowed. Anderson claimed it was the enemy's attempt at psychological warfare.

"Still alive?" Anderson asked, appearing with two steaming mugs.

"If that's your coffee, I'd rather not be," Stevenson replied.

Anderson raised an eyebrow. "Look, it's not that bad. You've got no taste."

"I used to. Then you burned it off."

They sipped in silence. The fog began to thin, and the outlines of tents and men moved into view like ghosts gathering for a meeting.

Rubert emerged from his tent, fully dressed, clean-shaven, and somehow already angry.

"Briefing in five. Bring your brains. Or borrow one."

Anderson leaned in. "That was his version of a good morning."

The briefing tent smelled of canvas, sweat, and the permanent tension of war.

Rubert stood by the map table, chewing on an unlit cigar. A young officer, jittery and too polished for fieldwork, stood beside him holding a file.

“New intel,” Rubert said. “French resistance intercepted German orders. There’s a hidden munitions depot just north of Marville.”

He stabbed a point on the map with a pencil.

“Your job: find it, confirm it, destroy it. Simple.”

Stevenson raised a brow. “What’s the catch, sir?”

Rubert looked up, that familiar steel in his eyes. “You’ll be going in light. On foot. Tanks stay behind. We need to keep the approach quiet.”

Anderson groaned. “You mean I have to walk?”

Rubert ignored him. “You’ll have one guide. French. Resistance contact. Rendezvous at this location,” he tapped again, “a barn two klicks from the border. You leave in twenty.”

As they left the tent, Stevenson nudged Anderson. “Ever worked with a resistance guide?”

Anderson shrugged. “Nope. But I’m hoping she’s not a man with bad breath and a machete.”

The barn looked like it had seen better centuries.

Its roof was a mosaic of broken tiles and hope. Inside, hay was piled high, and pigeons cooed from rafters like suspicious landlords. Stevenson scanned the shadows while Anderson poked around.

“I don’t like this,” Stevenson muttered.

“That’s because there’s no tank to hide in.”

A movement.

Then, from behind a haystack, stepped **Clara**.

Tall. Slender. A scarf tied in her dark brown hair. Mud-streaked boots. A pistol at her hip. And eyes—sharp, calculating, and far too tired for her age.

"You're late," she said, in fluent English.

Anderson opened his mouth but wisely shut it. For once, he couldn't find a joke.

Stevenson stepped forward. "You must be Clara. I'm—"

"Stevenson. And you're Anderson," she said. "The Americans who think enemy tanks explode just by looking at them."

Anderson smirked. "Well. Sometimes they do."

She motioned to the far end of the barn. "We move in five. The depot is hidden inside a wine cellar beneath an old hotel. Germans use the place for parties and lies."

Anderson grinned. "Sounds like my uncle's house."

Clara didn't smile. "If you get me killed, I'll haunt you."

"I welcome the company."

Stevenson pulled Anderson aside. "Can we not flirt with the resistance contact?"

"I wasn't flirting. I was bonding."

"Do it quietly."

The march to Marville took three hours.

The fog had burned off, and the landscape rolled out like a patchwork of ruin and rebirth. Trees lined the road, many scarred by bullets. Houses, roofless and abandoned, stood like crooked teeth in the hills.

Clara led them through paths Stevenson never would've found—along riverbanks, under fences, and through a field of sunflowers somehow untouched by war. Even Anderson walked quietly.

At last, they reached a ridge. Below, the town of Marville slept under a gray sky.

"There," Clara said, pointing to a grand old building near the center. "The hotel. Germans moved in last week. Four guards at the entrance, more inside."

Stevenson studied the layout. "We'll need a distraction."

Anderson pulled a grenade from his belt like a magician drawing a rabbit. "Always prepared."

"No," Clara snapped. "That's loud. We do this clean."

Stevenson glanced at her. "What do you suggest?"

She hesitated, then reached into her coat. Pulled out a **red ribbon**.

She tied it around her hair.

"Wait here."

And just like that, she walked down the slope toward the town like she belonged there.

Anderson leaned in. "Are we being rescued by a scarf?"

"She has a plan," Stevenson said.

"I'm starting to like her."

"Focus."

Clara reached the hotel gates without a single rifle raised.

The guards turned their heads. She said something in French. Laughed. Gestured to her bag.

One guard stepped forward.

Then another.

And that's when Stevenson and Anderson slipped in from the side, using the distraction to duck behind a cart and slide through the kitchen door. They moved silently, like ghosts trained in gunmetal.

Inside, the hotel smelled of wine, meat, and perfume—Germans living too well for men on the wrong side of history.

Anderson peered around corners. "Feels like a masquerade party."

"Keep your mask on," Stevenson whispered.

They found the cellar door near the pantry. Locked.

Anderson produced a small tool. "Learned this from a guy in Belgium. He owed me money."

Click.

Door opened.

The cellar was cold, damp, and reeked of mold. But there—behind wine racks and barrels—was the stash: crates of ammunition, grenades, rifles, and maps.

Stevenson placed charges.

“Two minutes,” he said.

As they turned to leave, they heard shouting above. German voices. Then, footsteps. Rapid.

“She’s in trouble,” Anderson hissed.

They burst through the kitchen as Clara was shoved back through the front door, hands raised, gun stripped from her belt.

Three soldiers. One held her by the arm.

Stevenson raised his weapon. “Let her go.”

One German shouted. A shot rang out.

Anderson’s bullet hit him between the eyes.

Chaos erupted.

Clara dove behind a pillar. Stevenson rolled and fired, hitting the second guard. Anderson tackled the third, a messy brawl that ended with the German out cold and Anderson bleeding from the lip.

They ran.

The explosion behind them lit up the hotel cellar like a volcano of steel and flame.

By nightfall, they were back at the barn.

Clara cleaned her arm—bruised but not broken. “Not bad for tank drivers.”

“You weren’t so bad for a woman with a ribbon,” Anderson said, then paused. “I meant that respectfully.”

Clara smirked. “If I’d known Americans were this charming, I’d have joined your army.”

Stevenson chuckled. “We pay terribly. And our coffee’s worse.”

She looked at him then, something softer in her eyes.

“I’m staying with your unit for now,” she said. “Rubert approved. He said you two need supervision.”

Anderson raised both eyebrows. “I love that man.”

Clara stood. “Get some sleep. Tomorrow, we fight again.”

As she walked away, Stevenson sat on a log, watching the flames of the small campfire flicker.

Anderson leaned back, hands behind his head.

“So,” he said, “still looking for a woman to marry?”

Stevenson didn’t answer immediately.

Then, quietly, “Maybe I just found one.”

Chapter 3: The Poet with a Rifle

The camp was stirring well before sunrise. The cold hadn't yet lifted, and soldiers moved like shadows through the mist, muffled in greatcoats and silence.

Stevenson sat outside his tent, sharpening a pocket knife against a whetstone with absent strokes. His mind wasn't on the blade—it was still at the barn, at the explosion, at Clara's ribbon swaying in the heat of danger.

She was awake too. He'd seen her an hour ago, already speaking with Rubert, already planning something. She was like that—wired tight and precise, like a clock that refused to tick off-beat.

Anderson emerged from the tent next door, hair wild and eyes half-closed.

"I dreamed a cow tried to marry me," he said, yawning. "I think it's your fault."

Stevenson didn't look up. "Was the cow French?"

"She wore lipstick. That's all I remember."

"Sounds like your type."

Anderson groaned and sat beside him. "You've got that quiet look. The one you wear right before we almost die."

"Rubert called a briefing. Something's up."

"Something's *always* up. That's what war is—something up, and we're sent to knock it down."

Rubert's tent was dim, lit only by a swinging lamp and a stack of half-crumpled maps. Clara stood beside him, arms folded, expression unreadable.

Rubert didn't waste time.

"Rail line east of Roucy. Germans are moving artillery by train. Resistance sabotaged one line—now they're using a backup route. We hit it tonight."

He pointed at a stretch of line running through a valley.

"Minimal guards, maybe a dozen. Blow the track, take the supplies, get out. You'll have backup this time."

Stevenson frowned. "Who's backup?"

Rubert turned toward the tent flap.

"Private Malley," he barked.

In stepped a boy who looked barely older than nineteen.

Private Oliver Malley saluted too quickly and tripped over the edge of the canvas. His rifle almost flew out of his hands.

Anderson blinked. "Sir… I think your backup brought his homework."

Malley's face flushed. "I'm trained, sir. Qualified sharpshooter. And… I write poetry in my downtime."

"Poetry?" Anderson asked, aghast. "That's what you do between bullets?"

"It helps me process trauma."

"It helps me judge you."

Rubert cleared his throat. Loudly.

"Malley's been assigned to your team. Treat him like any other soldier. He may be young, but he knows his way around a rifle. And a rhyme, apparently."

Clara gave Malley a small smile. "Can you follow orders?"

"Yes, ma'am."

"Then you're more useful than half the people I've worked with."

Anderson raised a finger. "Excuse me, I—"

"*Half*, Anderson," she said, before he could finish.

That evening, the four of them moved out on foot.

It wasn't raining, but it *smelled* like it would. The air was heavy, thick with the scent of wet grass and distant smoke. Malley walked in the rear, eyes darting between the trees, humming something quietly.

"What are you singing?" Stevenson asked.

"Not a song. A poem," Malley replied.

Anderson groaned. "Is there a version with gunfire in it?"

"No," Malley replied. "But I could write one."

"I'm going to regret this mission."

By midnight, they were crouched on a ridge overlooking the railway line. The valley below was quiet except for the chirping of crickets and the distant rattle of an approaching train.

Two guards paced beside a small shed near the tracks. Another sat on a supply crate, smoking and talking to himself.

Stevenson unfolded the small satchel of explosives. "We blow the bridge section as the train's crossing. Maximum impact. Minimum chase."

Clara pointed at the guards. “We take them out silently. I’ll circle left. You two—” she motioned to Anderson and Malley, “take the right.”

Malley nodded. His hands trembled slightly on the rifle.

“You good?” Stevenson asked.

“Better in poetry,” Malley admitted. “But I’ll manage.”

Anderson gave him a playful slap on the back. “Just pretend the guards are grammar mistakes.”

The approach was smooth—until it wasn’t.

Anderson crept behind the first guard like a cat.

Malley lined up the second one, breathing slow, finger tight on the trigger.

Then, the man on the crate sneezed loudly—and dropped his lantern.

The sound echoed.

The guards turned. One shouted. A gun was raised.

Malley shot first.

The guard spun and dropped. Then all hell broke loose.

Clara dashed forward, tackled the last guard and smashed the back of his head with the butt of her pistol. Anderson grabbed the smoking lantern and hurled it into the dark.

Stevenson, already halfway across the track, set the charges.

“Train in one minute!” he called.

They all sprinted.

The rumble of the train grew louder.

Clara pulled Malley up from where he'd stumbled on a rail. "Move!"

The moment they reached cover, Stevenson hit the detonator.

The explosion ripped the bridge apart.

The train leapt off the rails like a whale breaching the sea—and came crashing down in a magnificent fireball. Sparks flew. Metal shrieked. One of the cannons inside erupted as it hit the ground.

Anderson exhaled. "Now *that's* poetry."

Malley grinned. "Actually, that's *violence*. But I like your thinking."

They camped under a collapsed barn a few miles out. The fire burned low, smoke trailing into the starlight.

Malley scribbled into a small notebook.

Clara leaned over. "What are you writing?"

"A haiku."

Anderson laughed. “What kind of haiku fits this mess?”

Malley read:

Steel bird roars at night
Tracks devoured by orange flame
We walk home in ash.

Even Clara looked impressed.

Anderson blinked. “Huh. Still think it needs more explosions.”

Stevenson watched them all—the poet, the soldier, the resistance woman, his oddball best friend—and for the first time in a long while, felt like the war had brought him something other than destruction.

A strange little team. But his team.

Chapter 4: The Man in the Church Tower

Rain tapped softly on the tin roof of the outpost. Outside, the world was all grey mist and puddles. Inside, Stevenson was oiling his sidearm with the focus of a man trying to ignore a headache—or a heartache.

Clara had barely spoken since the train job.

She sat across the room, working on maps with Rubert. They leaned close, voices low. Strategic, yes. But maybe also... personal?

Anderson entered with a dripping coat and a face full of suspicion.

“She’s been in there with Rubert for an hour,” he muttered, handing Stevenson a steaming mug.

“Maybe they’re just planning,” Stevenson offered.

“Maybe. Or maybe he’s reciting love letters from Napoleon.”

Stevenson stared at the door.

Anderson nudged him. “Jealous?”

“No.”

Anderson leaned back with a grin. “That’s the most passionate 'no' I’ve heard all month.”

Before Stevenson could answer, Rubert emerged, serious as ever, followed by Clara who glanced once at Stevenson and said nothing.

Rubert wasted no time.

“We’ve got a problem,” he said. “There’s a German informant. Someone feeding troop locations to the enemy. Resistance has narrowed it down to three suspects in the village of Saint-Cyr.”

Anderson looked up. “You want us to knock on doors and say, ‘Hello, are you a traitor?’”

“No,” Rubert said. “You’re going undercover.”

Malley, who had just arrived with his rifle slung like a violin, perked up. “Like in disguise?”

“Exactly,” Rubert said. “You’ll pose as refugees. Clara will lead. Your job is to blend in, gather intel, and identify the spy.”

Stevenson frowned. “And when we find him?”

Rubert’s eyes darkened.

“Make sure he never finds anyone else.”

Saint-Cyr was a quiet village nestled between rolling hills and vineyards—too quiet. Half the buildings bore bullet holes. A few still smoldered from shelling a week earlier. Children watched from shuttered windows, their eyes too old for their faces.

Clara led the group through the main square, wrapped in a worn shawl. Stevenson carried a crate on his back. Malley held a bundle of blankets. Anderson, absurdly, wore a monocle he’d found in an abandoned trench.

“What are you doing?” Stevenson whispered.

“Disguise,” Anderson said. “I’m eccentric. People trust eccentric men.”

“They also shoot them faster.”

They settled in the church. The priest—a thin, quiet man named Father Henri—welcomed them with nods and warm soup. He said little. Mostly watched.

That night, while lightning cracked across the hills, Clara laid out the three suspects.

“First, Lucien—the innkeeper. Friendly, always asking questions.”

“Suspiciously friendly,” Anderson noted.

“Second, Emilie—the baker’s wife. She visits the German post every week. Claims she brings bread.”

“And maybe intel.”

“Third,” Clara said, “the bell keeper. Jean Vallot. Lives alone in the church tower. Never speaks. Always watching.”

Stevenson rubbed his chin. “Sounds like my uncle.”

Malley leaned in. “How do we figure out which one’s leaking information?”

Clara smiled thinly. “We stir the pot.”

The next day, Anderson “accidentally” left a map fragment at the inn. Malley dropped false whispers in the bakery. Clara delivered a basket to the bell tower with a coded note tucked under the bread. The bait was set.

That evening, Clara and Stevenson climbed the bell tower.

Jean Vallot was already there.

He was tall, stooped, and silent. His face was gaunt, like a man who hadn’t eaten or laughed in years. His eyes, pale and almost yellow, met theirs with an unsettling calm.

Clara handed over the bread. Jean took it without a word.

Stevenson tried friendly.

“Quiet view up here.”

No response.

“I suppose you get a good look at the village from here.”

Still nothing.

Then—just as they turned to leave—Jean spoke.

“War makes cowards of the honest and kings of liars.”

His voice was cracked. Ancient. Like gravel over bones.

Clara paused.

Stevenson frowned. “Are you saying you’re a coward or a king?”

Jean turned to the window, staring out at the grey world. “I ring the bell. I watch. I listen. And I bury my sins beneath the stones.”

They left in silence.

Back at the church, they found Anderson pacing.

“The innkeeper’s gone,” he said. “Packed up this afternoon. Told someone he was going hunting.”

“Hunting what?” Malley asked.

Anderson grinned. “That’s what I asked. He said, ‘Answers.’”

Clara tensed. “He took the bait.”

She pulled her pistol. “We find him. Now.”

The storm had grown worse by the time they reached the edge of the village. Wind lashed at their coats, and thunder rattled the sky.

In a ruined barn, they found him—**Lucien**, the innkeeper—rifling through a satchel by lamplight. He had a pistol, a radio, and the false map from the inn.

He didn't see them coming.

Clara fired a warning shot into the beam above him. "Step away."

Lucien raised his hands slowly. "You don't understand."

"Try us," Stevenson said.

Lucien looked between them. "I have a daughter. In Alsace. The Germans promised to keep her alive. If I gave them movement data. That's all I did."

"You sold men's lives for one," Clara said.

"I had no choice."

Malley looked at him, quiet and pale. "You always have a choice."

Lucien's eyes welled up. "They have my child."

Clara hesitated.

Anderson, too.

Stevenson stepped forward.

He looked Lucien in the eyes, then took the radio and crushed it underfoot.

"You're done," he said. "If they contact you again, you stall them. If they threaten her, we'll find her. But if you ever betray another soldier, I'll make sure your daughter remembers you as a traitor."

Lucien nodded, tears streaming down his face.

They left him there, under the storm, clutching a photograph and a shaking prayer.

Back at camp, Rubert heard the story without comment.

When Stevenson finished, the commander leaned back and took a long breath.

“Good call,” he said.

“You would’ve shot him,” Stevenson replied.

Rubert’s eyes flicked up. “That’s why I sent *you*.”

Outside, the sky cleared. The rain passed. For now.

Late that night, Clara sat beside Stevenson near the fire.

“He made the wrong choice,” she said. “But I understand why.”

Stevenson nodded.

“You did the right thing.”

She looked at him. “Would you do it for me? Choose me over the mission?”

Stevenson didn’t hesitate. “I’d make sure there was no choice to make.”

She smiled, soft and tired.

“I’m starting to believe you.”

Chapter 5: Rubert's Scar

The valley was quiet, too quiet. A kind of silence that pressed on the ears like pressure under deep water. It wasn't peaceful—it was a warning.

Stevenson adjusted the scope of his rifle and scanned the distant hills. Nothing but trees, rock, and a thin trail of smoke curling from a broken chimney in a ghosted village.

Anderson sat beside him on a crumbling wall, chewing something that may or may not have been real gum.

"You ever notice how before every ambush, the birds stop chirping?"

Stevenson lowered the scope. "I think they're smarter than us."

"Yeah, they fly away. We walk in."

Below, Rubert paced along a trench carved in the hillside, barking short commands to a new squad. Clara was beside him, clipboard in hand, not looking up.

Today's mission wasn't like the others. It wasn't sabotage. It wasn't stealth.

It was **retaliation**.

Last night, a German patrol hit a resistance convoy near Vailly. Eight dead, three captured, including a courier with critical intel. Rubert knew what that meant: the enemy now had locations, maps, codes.

They had to strike before the Germans used it.

The plan was simple: ambush the returning patrol at a narrow gorge called **Wolf's Mouth**.

Rubert gathered the team under a mossy rock overhang.

“This will be fast and brutal,” he said. “They’ll be expecting a clear road. We’ll give them hell instead.”

Anderson raised a hand. “On a scale of one to ‘run screaming,’ how bad is it if this goes wrong?”

Rubert smiled grimly. “If this goes wrong, you won’t have time to run.”

The gorge was narrow and flanked by cliffs. The unit was split into three teams:

- **Rubert** and **Clara** at the top ridge, armed with scoped rifles and grenades.
- **Stevenson**, **Anderson**, and **Malley** on the opposite ledge with a mounted machine gun.
- A small group of resistance fighters hidden in the lower pass, waiting to block the road after the first hit.

Then… the sound came. The low growl of engines. Not one, but four trucks.

Stevenson took position behind the machine gun. His breath slowed.

Anderson peeked through binoculars.

“Five… six… ten Germans. Maybe more in the back trucks.”

Malley steadied his rifle. “I’ve got rear tires. Give me the signal.”

“Wait for Rubert.”

Atop the cliff, Rubert counted silently. One hand clenched tight on a grenade. Clara beside him, eyes narrowed.

As the second truck reached the marked blast point, Rubert whispered, “Now.”

The explosion was thunder in a canyon.

The first truck flipped. The second jackknifed into a boulder. Screams echoed up the stone walls.

Gunfire erupted from both sides. Anderson worked the machine gun like an organist at a death concert.

Malley fired clean. Two, three Germans dropped in quick succession.

The resistance fighters blocked the exit with a smoke charge and began firing from the cover of fallen logs.

The trap was working.

Then the third truck's canvas cover flapped open—and a mounted machine gun inside returned fire.

Anderson ducked as bullets tore into the stone beside him.

“That's cheating!” he yelled.

Stevenson adjusted. “Malley, we need a shot into the truck’s fuel tank!”

Malley nodded, adjusted… then flinched. His rifle jammed.

“I—I'm clearing it!”

“Too late!” Anderson shouted.

Stevenson grabbed a grenade, yanked the pin, and hurled it with all the power in his arms.

It landed under the third truck.

The explosion sent burning tires into the sky. A second wave of screams followed.

But not all of them German.

Down below, one of the resistance fighters was hit.

Clara saw him fall, his body crumpling beside a blackened log. She cursed under her breath and stood.

“Cover me!” she shouted, and sprinted.

Rubert barked, “No—Clara!”

But she was already sliding down the ridge.

Rubert watched as she reached the wounded man. She dragged him back, bullets striking dirt around her boots.

At that moment, something snapped in Rubert. Not a commander's calculation—something older. Something buried.

Later that night, when the fight was done and the fires died out, Stevenson found Rubert alone near a broken stone altar in the village church.

The commander sat on a bench, his greatcoat stained with mud and blood. In his hand was a small, rusted pocket watch.

Stevenson sat down beside him.

Rubert didn’t speak right away. When he did, his voice was flat.

“You know I fought in the last war.”

“I figured.”

Rubert nodded. “Verdun. 1916. I was nineteen. They told us we were saving France.”

Stevenson waited.

"We held a trench for eight days. No food. No ammo. Just mud and bones. I watched friends die in ways that shouldn't be possible."

He opened the pocket watch. Inside was a tiny photo—faded, water-damaged.

A young woman, holding a baby.

"My wife. Geneviève. And our daughter, Elise."

Stevenson blinked. "I didn't know you had a family."

"I don't," Rubert said. "Not anymore."

"What happened?"

Rubert exhaled. "When the trench fell, they took me prisoner. I was gone six months. When I came back, my village had been bombed. My house was gone. So were they."

He looked at Stevenson.

"That's the scar I carry. Not the ones on my body—the ones no one sees."

Stevenson swallowed. "That's why you fight."

Rubert shook his head. "No. That's why I lead. So no one else has to carry what I carry."

They sat in silence for a long time.

Then Rubert added, quietly, "Clara reminds me of her. My daughter. Brave. Stubborn. Smarter than I ever was."

Later, as the team gathered around a low fire, tending wounds and swapping stories, Malley pulled out his notebook.

"I wrote a line," he said. "About today."

Anderson rolled his eyes. “Let me guess: ‘Kaboom, kabang, we saved the day’?”

Malley smiled.

“No. It’s about scars.”

He read:

Some scars are loud—like fire and steel,
But others live where no eyes feel.
The pain that hides behind a name,
Is not less real because it came—
Without a wound.

Even Anderson was quiet.

Clara reached over and touched Malley’s arm. “That’s a good line.”

Rubert didn’t speak. But he nodded once.

Chapter 6: The House by the River

The orders were clear: “Evacuate the civilians before the Germans reach Pont du Foudre.”

But the situation on the ground was far from clear.

Pont du Foudre—Thunder Bridge—was a small stone village tucked beside the Yvette River. Just thirty homes, a bakery, a smithy, and a monastery with bells that hadn’t rung in years. According to resistance scouts, a German detachment was moving fast from the east, burning villages suspected of harboring Allied sympathizers. Pont du Foudre was next.

Rubert's team had twelve hours.

“Why is it always raining?” Anderson muttered as they trudged through a muddy field.

Stevenson wiped his brow. “It’s France. The clouds are patriotic.”

Anderson grinned. “Then someone tell France to declare sunshine.”

Malley, behind them, chuckled.

They reached the village just after sunrise. It was still asleep, unaware that death was marching toward it in steel boots.

Rubert ordered the squad to split up.

“Go house to house. No arguments. Everyone leaves. If they resist, remind them what happened at Verelle.”

Clara added, “We have three wagons and limited time. Pack light. Prioritize the elderly and children.”

Anderson leaned over to Stevenson. “You notice how she sounds more like a commander every day?”

“She’s more convincing than most,” Stevenson replied.

He didn’t say how proud of her he felt. Or how she had started appearing in his thoughts without invitation.

House to house they went. Some villagers listened. Some cried. A few cursed them.

One old woman refused to leave without her cow.

“No,” Anderson said. “Cows don’t count as family.”

“She is my *daughter* now,” the woman insisted.

Stevenson gently intervened. “Madame, we have children to save. The cow stays.”

“But she makes wonderful cheese—”

“Then may she rest in dairy heaven.”

By late afternoon, the convoy was almost ready.

But Clara was missing.

Rubert sent Stevenson and Malley to find her. They combed the narrow alleys until they reached a weathered house on the river’s edge.

Stevenson pushed the door open.

Inside, Clara knelt beside a young girl, maybe eight years old, hiding under a table. A wounded man—likely the girl’s father—lay on a mattress, his leg bandaged and blood-soaked.

"I can't leave them," Clara said. "He can't move."

Stevenson entered slowly. "Clara, we have twenty minutes. The wagons are full."

"Then we make space."

Stevenson looked at the man. One look told him everything.

"He's not going to survive the trip."

"I'm not leaving them," she repeated, eyes blazing.

Malley stepped forward. "I'll carry him."

"Malley—"

"I'm not letting another kid grow up an orphan if I can help it."

With a grunt, Malley lifted the man over his shoulder. The child clung to Clara's hand.

They were nearly to the wagons when they heard it: the hum of trucks in the distance. Then the distinct metallic clink of tank treads.

"They're early," Rubert snapped. "Move! Now!"

Stevenson and Clara rushed the girl into the last wagon. Malley collapsed behind them, the wounded man slipping from his arms.

Rubert shouted, "Go! Go!"

The convoy pulled out just as German forces crested the far hill. Gunfire barked.

Stevenson and Clara jumped into the last cart. Anderson, up front, cracked the reins.

The girl was crying, curled against Clara.

“They didn’t fire warning shots,” Clara whispered.

“They weren’t meant to warn,” Rubert growled. “They were meant to kill.”

They lost one wagon. A shell struck the rear cart, killing the driver instantly. Two passengers jumped and ran into the woods—only one made it out.

Malley caught shrapnel in his shoulder. Anderson took the reins of both remaining carts and drove like a demon through fog and mud.

Stevenson covered them from the back, firing at shadows that moved too fast.

Finally, they reached a bend in the road where the Resistance had planted mines.

Rubert detonated them.

A wall of fire and earth blocked the German pursuit—for now.

That night, under a tarp stretched between two wagons, the survivors rested.

The little girl curled up beside Clara, finally asleep. The man was dead. Malley’s wound was wrapped.

Anderson smoked a crushed cigar, eyes half-closed. “I liked the cow,” he muttered.

Rubert checked on the group, his usual steel cracking slightly. He put a hand on Stevenson’s shoulder.

“You did good.”

Stevenson didn't reply.

Later, when most had drifted off, he found Clara sitting by the riverbank, staring at the moon's reflection.

"You did the right thing," he said.

"Feels like I left half of me behind."

He sat beside her.

"You saved her. That's enough for one day."

They sat in silence, listening to the water.

Then she whispered, "I was scared. More scared than I've ever been."

He turned to her. "So was I."

They looked at each other.

And for a long moment, the war receded—the noise, the fire, the weight of death. There was only the night, and them, and a fragile breath of peace.

Chapter 7: Shadows in the Firelight

The camp was unusually quiet.

After the harrowing escape from Pont du Foudre, the squad had found shelter in the ruins of a burnt-out vineyard nestled between the hills. Grapevines still clung to the blackened trellises like ghosts of the past. There was water, shelter, and—for once—no bullets.

Rubert paced the edge of the firelight, sharpening his blade on a stone that had survived both wars. He hadn’t spoken much since the escape. His silence, unlike Anderson’s wisecracks or Clara’s focused calm, carried the weight of worry.

Stevenson watched him from across the fire.

“Something’s wrong,” he said to Clara.

She glanced over. “You noticed too?”

“He’s been reading that coded dispatch over and over again.”

Anderson, lying on his back with a twig between his teeth, joined in without opening his eyes. “Maybe it’s a love letter. ‘Dear Rubert, I think your sword is sexy. Meet me at sunset—bring explosives.’”

Malley chuckled, even while cleaning the wound on his shoulder.

Rubert’s voice cut through the humor. “We have a problem.”

Everyone sat up.

He held up the piece of paper. “Intercepted message. Resistance says a German officer is defecting. He has high-level intel. But—” he folded the paper slowly “—someone in our ranks is sending out counter-signals.”

“A mole?” Stevenson asked.

Rubert nodded. “And they’re trying to stop the meeting.”

The message gave a single coordinate: *Les Trois Chênes*—The Three Oaks. A half-collapsed chapel near the border. The defector would arrive in three days.

Anderson squinted at the map. “It’s a two-day trek through enemy-held forest, booby-trapped with mines, wolves, and worse—snipers with no sense of humor.”

Clara looked at Rubert. “We can’t split the squad, not with a mole among us.”

“Exactly,” Rubert replied. “We stay together. We move quiet. We trust no one fully.”

And then, he said the words no one wanted to hear.

“Even among ourselves.”

The forest swallowed them the next morning.

Rain turned the path to mush. The air smelled like wet bark and regret. Every snapped twig sounded like a pistol cocking.

Anderson tried to break the tension.

“You know, I used to camp like this when I was twelve.”

Clara looked back. “Did those camps also involve landmines?”

“Only if you stepped on my brother’s squirrel traps.”

Malley snorted. “Poor squirrels.”

“Poor me. Got caught in one. Didn’t sit for a week.”

Even Rubert cracked a brief grin.

But Stevenson stayed focused. He'd noticed something strange since the last skirmish—**Malley was asking too many questions**.

Not just about their path or the mission, but personal things. Backgrounds. Habits. Password phrases.

He kept his thoughts to himself. For now.

That night, they camped beneath a rock overhang, hidden from above by a canopy of thick moss. Anderson took first watch. Clara curled into her blanket near the fire. Malley cleaned his gun too meticulously.

Stevenson sat beside Rubert.

"Could be Malley."

Rubert didn't blink. "Could be any of us."

Stevenson hesitated. "Not Clara. I'd bet my life."

Rubert looked at him. "Are you sure you're not already betting it?"

Stevenson didn't answer.

Around midnight, movement rustled the bushes near the camp.

Anderson was already up, pistol drawn.

"Friend or foe, come out with hands up and pants on."

A figure emerged.

Skinny. Shivering. Barefoot. A young man with a bloodied French armband.

"My name is **Luc Morel**," he gasped. "I'm with the Resistance."

Rubert stepped forward cautiously. “How did you find us?”

“They’re coming,” Luc said. “The defector—he was captured. They know you’re heading to Les Trois Chênes. You’ve been betrayed.”

Rubert’s eyes narrowed. “By who?”

Luc pointed at Malley.

The fire seemed to flicker in time with everyone's breath.

Malley stood, his voice calm. “That’s a lie.”

Stevenson leveled his weapon. “Then prove it.”

“I don’t have to. He’s the one showing up out of nowhere.”

Luc shouted, “I saw him! Two nights ago, radioing coordinates to the Germans. I was following him. He tried to kill me.”

Clara looked from one man to the other. “Someone’s lying. But who?”

Tension stretched like a tripwire.

Then Anderson stepped forward.

“Let’s settle this like gentlemen,” he said. “One bullet in the chamber. Whoever’s lying, let fate decide.”

Rubert growled. “This isn’t a tavern duel, Anderson.”

“I’m kidding. Mostly.”

Stevenson stepped between Luc and Malley.

“Luc says he saw Malley. But Luc could be a plant, too.”

Rubert made a decision. “We tie them both. At dawn, we move. Whoever the traitor is, they’ll reveal themselves soon enough.”

But fate moved faster than dawn.

At 3 a.m., the first shot rang out.

Stevenson jolted awake.

Luc was dead, a bullet through his throat.

Malley was gone.

And the squad’s map was missing.

Rubert cursed. “He bought our trust, waited for doubt to break us, and vanished.”

Clara knelt over Luc’s body. “He told the truth.”

Anderson looked out into the dark woods. “Which means Malley’s heading straight to the Germans—with everything.”

Stevenson clenched his fists. “He knows the defector’s meeting point. He’ll be waiting there when the man arrives.”

Rubert nodded grimly. “Then so will we.”

Chapter 8: The Three Oaks

Dawn did not break gently.

It came with wind that howled through the ravines, tugging at cloaks and snapping branches. The forest turned gray. Trees loomed like watchmen. Somewhere in the vast cold beyond, Malley was running—faster than them, with knowledge he shouldn't have had.

Rubert ordered a forced march. No breakfast. No small talk.

"Three Oaks by dusk," he said. "Or the mission dies."

Stevenson had never hated trees until now. The forest seemed to repeat itself endlessly: a cruel loop of branches and shadows. No birds, no sign of animals. Even the silence felt staged, like something—or someone—was listening.

Anderson tried to joke.

"If Malley's smart, he'll sprain his ankle on a tree root and limp into a bear's den."

Clara, walking beside Stevenson, shook her head. "He's smart. That's the problem."

Stevenson added, "He knew how we moved. Our signals. Even our fallback routes."

Anderson grunted. "And he played dumb about everything. I should've known. He once asked me how to disassemble a German MP40. Who doesn't know that?"

Rubert interrupted. "He's not working alone."

That made them all stop.

"What do you mean?" Clara asked.

Rubert didn't slow down. "He had a backup. Someone who helped plant Luc's body, stage the escape. Someone who passed him information."

Anderson raised an eyebrow. "You think there's still another mole?"

"I don't think. I know."

By midday, the squad reached a ridge. Below them sprawled the **Les Trois Chênes chapel**—once a sanctuary, now a stone skeleton. The three great oak trees stood nearby, twisted and gnarled by time, like giants frozen mid-battle.

Smoke curled faintly from behind the chapel.

"Campfire," Clara whispered.

"Too early for the defector," Stevenson said.

Rubert pulled out binoculars. "One person. Malley."

Anderson patted his rifle. "Let me get reacquainted with him."

"No. If he's waiting for us, he's baiting us," Rubert replied. "He wants us to come crashing in."

They crouched behind the ridge to plan.

The approach had to be silent.

Rubert would circle from the left through the brush. Clara and Stevenson would go straight through the broken wall. Anderson would climb a crumbled bell tower for cover.

As the group split up, Anderson grinned. “If I fall from this tower, I want you to lie to my mother. Tell her I died doing something manly, like wrestling a German panther.”

Stevenson rolled his eyes. “Noted.”

Inside the chapel, it was cold and hollow. Pews were broken. Sunlight filtered through cracked stained glass in splinters of red and blue.

Malley sat alone by the fire, polishing a pistol like a man cleaning his conscience.

“You’re late,” he called without turning. “I was hoping you’d show up before the guest arrives.”

Stevenson stepped forward. “You killed Luc. Gave up your team. Why?”

Malley didn’t flinch. “Because I stopped believing in stories. In heroes. In any of it.”

Clara emerged behind a pillar. “You could’ve just walked away.”

“I did. And I took the truth with me.”

Stevenson raised his gun. “Truth?”

“The war’s already lost,” Malley said. “Not the one out there. The one inside you. You don’t realize it yet, but they’ve already won.”

Then he stood, tossing the pistol into the fire.

Rubert appeared behind him, silent as smoke.

“You’re not walking away from this one.”

Malley looked over his shoulder. “No. I’m not.”

That's when the **first explosion** went off.

From the ridge.

Anderson's position.

The bell tower shuddered. Part of it collapsed.

Clara screamed, "ANDERSON!"

Rubert shoved Malley forward. "He set a trap!"

Stevenson bolted toward the tower, leaping over the ruins, ignoring the debris.

Anderson was bleeding, pinned under a beam, half-conscious.

"Don't you dare die here," Stevenson muttered, lifting the beam with all the strength he had.

Anderson coughed. "I said a panther, not a church."

They dragged him out as German voices echoed through the trees.

Clara checked her watch. "Fifteen minutes. The defector will be here."

Rubert turned to Malley. “Where are they coming from? What did you tell them?”

Malley smiled, blood trickling from his lip. “That you’re exactly where they want you.”

Gunfire lit up the edges of the forest.

A dozen German soldiers burst from the brush, fanning toward the chapel.

Rubert threw down a smoke grenade. “Fall back to the oaks!”

They ran.

Stevenson half-carried Anderson. Clara shot behind them with perfect aim.

They reached the largest oak—the one with a hollow base.

Inside it was a narrow root cellar, covered in old stone. Rubert kicked it open. “In!”

They tumbled inside.

Gunfire ripped through the tree moments later.

Inside the hidden chamber, it was pitch black, save for a sliver of light from above.

Anderson groaned. “If this is what heaven looks like, I’m unimpressed.”

Then a voice spoke from the shadows.

“You are not late, and that is good.”

A man emerged, wrapped in an old trench coat, face gaunt, eyes sharp.

“I am **Matthias Kroll**,” he said. “Former intelligence officer. I believe you are here for me.”

Chapter 9: The Man Who Knew Too Much

The cellar beneath the great oak was still and damp, smelling of old wine and older secrets.

Matthias Kroll stood before them like a shadow that had walked straight out of history. He was tall but frail, with pale skin that looked untouched by sunlight for years. His eyes—gray, sharp, and haunting—scanned each of them with the precision of a man used to reading danger between heartbeats.

Rubert raised his rifle. “Matthias Kroll?”

“Yes,” the man said, voice dry but composed. “And you must be the Americans who almost ruined this rendezvous.”

“You’re welcome,” Anderson grunted from the ground, blood trickling down his forehead. “Sorry we didn’t bring cookies.”

Matthias gave him a ghost of a smile.

Once the trapdoor was sealed again, and the muffled sounds of the German patrol faded into silence, they regrouped.

Clara began tending to Anderson’s wounds with quiet efficiency. Stevenson and Rubert sat opposite Kroll, keeping their weapons close.

“You’re risking your life to defect,” Rubert said. “What do you have that’s worth all this?”

Matthias replied calmly, “The location and schedule of every armored movement across the Western Front for the next six weeks. The plans for the Ardennes push. The names of informants in the Allied ranks. And a list of those Hitler plans to purge—friends and enemies alike.”

The room went quiet.

Anderson blinked. “So... just a little useful, then.”

Stevenson frowned. “Why defect now?”

Matthias looked down. “Because my conscience has become louder than my orders. I watched too many innocents vanish for causes I no longer believed in. My brother was executed for criticizing Himmler. My father was disappeared. I’ve had enough.”

He paused, then added, “Also, your side has better coffee.”

Anderson gave a weak thumbs-up from the corner. “He’s one of us now.”

Rubert nodded. “Alright. We move at dawn. First light gives us cover. We’ll circle east, past the river, and meet the extraction team near Mont Vire.”

But Clara raised a hand.

“There’s a problem. We still don’t know if Malley gave them more than the chapel location. If he knew about our fallback plan…”

“Then they’ll be waiting at Mont Vire too,” Stevenson said grimly.

That night, while the others rested or sharpened knives, Stevenson found Clara sitting alone at the mouth of the cellar. Moonlight filtered through the cracks above, painting her face in slivers of silver.

“You always find the best brooding spots,” he said, settling beside her.

She didn’t smile. “Too many near-deaths lately.”

Stevenson looked at her. “I meant to ask… back at the river, when we were hiding from the convoy. You said you’d never been that scared.”

“I haven’t.”

He hesitated. “And now?”

She turned to him. “Now, I’m not scared of dying. I’m scared of not making it out with the right people.”

Silence.

Then she added softly, “You’re one of the right people.”

His breath caught.

He reached for her hand.

For a long moment, their fingers touched but didn’t hold.

Then Clara turned away, gently pulling her hand back.

“Not yet,” she whispered. “Let’s survive first.”

The next morning, they moved out before the sun touched the hills.

Anderson limped but refused to be carried. “If I’m going down, I’m going down dramatically.”

Matthias led them through a hidden path—a dry riverbed that hadn’t flowed since spring. Rubert took the rear. Clara walked near the center, keeping a protective eye on both Kroll and Anderson.

It was Stevenson who saw the glint first.

High on the ridge—**a sniper's scope**.

"Down!" he shouted, shoving Clara aside just as a shot cracked the silence.

The bullet struck the stone beside her head, shattering it into dust.

Rubert fired back instantly. "AMBUSH!"

Matthias dove behind a rock. Anderson dragged himself behind a tree. Clara rolled and returned fire, quick as lightning.

They were pinned.

Rubert barked into his field radio. "Mayday! Squad under fire near Dead River Ridge! Repeat—under fire!"

The static crackled back. Then: "Hold position. Extraction in four minutes."

"Four minutes is a lifetime here," Clara muttered, firing another shot.

Stevenson turned to Anderson. "Got a grenade?"

Anderson handed one over. "Birthday present. Don't waste it."

Stevenson kissed the top of his helmet. "You're the best."

"Tell that to my next wife."

Stevenson crept along the riverbed's edge and launched the grenade up the ridge.

Boom.

Screams. Scrambling.

One sniper slid down the rocks, unconscious or worse.

Moments later, a low roar filled the valley.

A twin-prop American evac plane skimmed the ridge, dropping a rope ladder into the clearing beyond the trees.

“Go, go!” Rubert yelled.

They sprinted—or stumbled—toward it.

Stevenson helped Anderson up. Clara and Rubert flanked Matthias.

Bullets zipped past.

Clara turned mid-run and dropped the last German gunner with a clean shot to the neck.

They reached the clearing.

The rope ladder dangled like a miracle.

Anderson went first, muttering, “Don’t look down, don’t fart, don’t look down...”

Clara followed.

Matthias climbed with the desperation of a man who had already lived three lifetimes.

Rubert and Stevenson covered the rear.

Another shot rang out.

Rubert fell.

“NO!” Stevenson turned, firing wildly into the trees.

Rubert, bleeding but conscious, waved him off. “Climb. That's an order.”

"I'm not leaving you."

"Yes, you are."

Rubert shoved him toward the ladder with his last strength.

Stevenson hesitated—then obeyed.

As the plane rose, the world below shrank. Smoke. Blood. Shadows.

Rubert raised his hand in salute as the trees swallowed him whole.

Inside the plane, it was silent.

Clara sobbed quietly into her sleeve.

Anderson stared blankly ahead.

Stevenson sat beside Kroll, hands shaking.

Matthias leaned in and said, "That man saved more lives in his last hour than most do in a lifetime."

Stevenson didn’t speak.

But he believed it.

Chapter 10: Ghosts in Uniform

The extraction plane flew low over the French countryside, slicing through early morning mist like a silent blade. The world below was gray and distant now. The only sounds inside were the hum of the engine and the unspoken weight of what they'd just left behind.

Stevenson stared at the landscape through the narrow window, jaw clenched. Rubert's last salute still burned in his memory. That final shove. The order he couldn't refuse.

Clara sat across from him, her arms wrapped tightly around her knees. Anderson had finally passed out from exhaustion and pain, muttering something about whiskey and waffles.

Matthias Kroll sat upright and unnervingly still, as if he'd never been more at home than on a vibrating military aircraft heading toward uncertainty.

They landed on a remote Allied airfield in southern England, far from any front lines. Rain had turned the landing strip to mud, but no one cared.

Waiting on the tarmac was a tall, thin man in a long coat, hair slicked back, clipboard in hand: **Agent Cyril Foxworth**, MI6 liaison, and the very definition of "unimpressed."

“Lieutenant Stevenson,” he said without looking up from his notes. “Sergeant Anderson. Miss Clara Jules. Welcome back. Regretfully, you are the only ones.”

Stevenson frowned. “What do you mean?”

“We were expecting Commander Rubert.”

Clara turned away.

Foxworth continued coolly, “Ah. Then the reports were accurate.”

Anderson, groggy and bloodied, gave a sour laugh. “Well, aren’t you just a ray of bloody sunshine.”

Foxworth raised an eyebrow. “Apologies. We have much to debrief.”

The debriefing was long and full of acronyms.

They were ushered into a steel-walled room under the airstrip’s command tower. Tea was poured. Questions were fired.

Matthias laid everything on the table: maps, codes, names, and secrets that made even the senior officers go pale. He described troop deployments, weapons caches, and a new kind of communication technology the Germans were preparing to launch—a system that could intercept Allied messages in real-time.

And then came the bombshell.

"There is someone embedded high in Allied command," Kroll said. "An informant. A mole. I don't know his name, but his code is **Black Hyena**. He feeds your movements to the Wehrmacht."

Silence fell.

Stevenson looked at Clara. Her lips were pressed tight.

Anderson finally muttered, "First a rat in our squad, now one in the whole damn cheese wheel."

After the debriefing, the trio was given temporary quarters in an abandoned manor near the airfield. Beds. Real food. And for the first time in weeks—privacy.

Stevenson walked through the cold stone halls, unsure what to do with himself. He ended up in the library, thumbing through a dusty copy of *King Solomon's Mines*.

Clara found him there, hours later.

"I thought you'd be asleep," she said.

He looked up. "Can't. Everything's too quiet. Too clean. Doesn't feel real."

She stepped closer. "Do you think Rubert's still alive?"

He exhaled slowly. "If anyone could survive an ambush with a bullet in their leg and a dozen men behind him—it's him."

Clara nodded, then sat beside him.

“You know,” she said, voice soft, “I told myself after the war, I’d open a flower shop. Someplace quiet. No guns. No uniforms. Just sun and petals.”

Stevenson smiled. “I pictured a diner. Maybe in Texas. Run by an old lady who always calls you ‘darlin’ and serves bacon that could stop your heart.”

She smiled back. “You should come to the flower shop sometime.”

“Only if you serve coffee.”

Clara reached over and gently took his hand. This time, she didn’t let go.

Down the hall, Anderson snored so loudly it echoed through the vents.

In his room, he'd laid out a map on his bed, scribbling sarcastic notes in the margins.

Under *Possible Mole Suspects*, he’d written:

- General Pompous (Probably allergic to honesty)
- Major Scowlface (Never trusts a man with jokes)
- Me (But I’m too handsome to betray)

The next morning, Foxworth returned with news.

“We’re moving you,” he said. “To London. We need you near command. Kroll’s information suggests another major German offensive, perhaps in the Ardennes.”

Stevenson frowned. “What about the mole?”

Foxworth looked uneasy. “We’re investigating. But discretion is critical. You’re being reassigned to **Operation Glass Dagger**.”

"Glass what?" Anderson asked, rubbing sleep from his eyes.

"A counter-intelligence unit tasked with baiting out Black Hyena," Foxworth explained. "You'll be given false plans—convincing, but fake. If those plans leak to the enemy, we'll know who passed them."

Clara's eyes narrowed. "You're using us as bait."

"Better bait than bodies," Foxworth replied coldly. "But you'll have backup. You'll operate under new aliases."

He handed them their new papers.

Anderson opened his and burst out laughing. "*Arnold Buttercup?* What am I, a pastry chef?"

Clara read hers. "*Margaret Tinsley.* That sounds like a woman who bakes regret into her pies."

Stevenson flipped his own.

"*Peter Holloway*," he muttered. "Sounds... normal."

"Perfect," said Foxworth.

That evening, before their train to London, Stevenson found Clara again—this time in the manor's overgrown garden.

"I'm not used to aliases," he said. "I barely remember who I was before this war."

Clara plucked a dying rose from a bush. "Then let's not pretend to be them. Holloway and Tinsley can play spies. But you and I—Stevenson and Clara—we stay who we are."

He smiled. "Deal."

Then she surprised him.

She leaned in and kissed him—gently, steadily, and without apology.

When she pulled back, she whispered, “For good luck.”

And just like that, the shadows lifted—just a little.

Chapter 11: Holloway, Tinsley, and the Trapdoor to Treason

The London safe house was disguised as an old tailor’s shop in Bloomsbury, tucked between a bakery and a tobacconist. Inside, the air smelled of chalk, wool, and secrets. Outside, the city groaned beneath the weight of wartime pressure—sirens, blackouts, and ration queues that wrapped around blocks like hungry snakes.

For Stevenson, now “Peter Holloway,” it was the beginning of a game he never wanted to play: not of bullets, but of whispers and eyes in mirrors.

Foxworth was already waiting in the shop’s back room. He pushed his glasses up the bridge of his nose and gestured to the table.

“Sit. Time for your first assignment under Glass Dagger.”

Stevenson sat. Clara—now “Margaret Tinsley”—took the seat beside him, legs crossed, sharp eyes scanning the room like a practiced spy. Anderson slumped into a chair opposite them, balancing a teacup on his knee.

Foxworth laid out the forged intelligence packet. It looked real enough: maps marked with troop routes, ciphered coordinates, and a fabricated plan to move Allied forces through a "weak" corridor in the Ardennes.

"We leak this through a controlled channel," Foxworth said. "If the Germans act on it, we know the leak is from here. And we'll know who had access."

Stevenson nodded slowly. "And if the mole realizes it's bait?"

"Then we'll have to get creative," Foxworth replied. "Which brings us to your next cover assignments."

He handed out slips of paper.

Anderson squinted. "*I'm a pub singer named Tommy Bristlefist?*"

Foxworth deadpanned. "You'll work out of a known meeting spot for covert messages. Your act is the distraction. Your ears are the real tool."

Clara looked up from hers. "*I'm a cryptologist for the Ministry of Supply.* Not bad."

Stevenson read his. "*Driver for military dispatch office.* Huh."

Anderson grinned. "You get to wear gloves and complain about potholes. Jealous."

The next day, they began their roles.

Anderson spent his nights belting out sea shanties in a smoky pub called *The Limping Stag*, where his voice, surprisingly passable, earned him a small fanbase and several pints per hour. Between choruses, he eavesdropped on conversations, memorizing code names, and occasionally planting misinformation.

Clara sat in a gray government building with clacking typewriters and suspicious glances. Her job was decoding messages—real and fake. She passed occasional reports through a secure chute to Foxworth's office, always watching to see who paid attention.

Stevenson drove officers and parcels around the city, absorbing routes, overhearing gossip, and pretending to be dumber than he was. He carried a notebook in his pocket titled *Oil Changes and Other Miseries*, which actually contained shorthand notes on every passenger who asked odd questions or sniffed too often.

One rainy evening, Clara returned to the safe house with an urgent face.

"I think someone's onto us," she whispered. "There was a man—tall, mustache, trench coat—watching the entrance. He didn't follow me, but he wasn't a passerby either."

Anderson looked up from his toast. "Tall, mustache? Did he look like someone who collects stamps or someone who collects ears?"

"More like someone who could do both," she replied.

Foxworth arrived twenty minutes later, breathless.

"We have movement. The false Ardennes intel? Someone used it."

Stevenson sat up. "Already?"

Foxworth nodded. "A transmission was intercepted by the RAF—details of the fake plan, sent to Berlin using an obsolete cipher. Only six people had access to it, all within our circle."

Anderson leaned back. "So it's one of us. Not *us*, us. Hopefully."

Foxworth dropped a list on the table. Six names.

Stevenson read through it and paused on the last one: **Commander Rubert**.

He froze. "Why is Rubert's name on this?"

Foxworth looked grim. “Because he’s alive. And he’s been seen near Berlin.”

Silence.

Anderson’s face hardened. “That’s not possible. He stayed behind to cover us. He—he *died*.”

Clara shook her head. “They never confirmed his body, did they?”

Stevenson stared at the name, mind spinning. “If Rubert’s alive... and helping them...”

“No,” Clara whispered. “He wouldn’t.”

Foxworth held up his hands. “Let’s not jump to conclusions. We’ve asked for aerial photographs. If it *is* Rubert, he may be a double agent, brainwashed, or worse. But right now, he’s our only link to Black Hyena.”

The next day brought a new assignment.

“You’re going to a gala,” Foxworth announced.

Anderson’s eyebrows climbed. “What is this, *Espionage: The Musical*?”

“British Intelligence is hosting an officers’ ball for American and French liaisons,” Foxworth explained. “It’s a perfect place for the mole to pass or collect information.”

Stevenson grimaced. “And what’s our role?”

“Observe. Blend. Dance, if you must. But eyes open. One of the six suspects will be there.”

He passed out new IDs.

Clara laughed. “*Lady Eleanor Aberbridge?* Well, well.”

Anderson snorted. “Mine says *Captain Reginald Teacup*. This is sabotage.”

Stevenson flipped his open. “*Major Charles Penwell.* Hmm. Sounds like a man who polishes his buttons twice a day.”

That evening, they stepped into the marble-lit world of the MI6 gala. Polished boots, gold epaulettes, flowing gowns, and eyes sharper than bayonets.

Clara glided through the room with practiced elegance, pausing by officers with champagne and subtle questions. Stevenson stuck close to the bar, scanning faces. Anderson floated like smoke, chatting up colonels and dancing with secretaries.

Then, Stevenson saw him.

Across the room. Near the back.

Rubert.

Wearing a civilian coat, but unmistakably him—same jawline, same scar above the brow.

He was speaking with a British general. Laughing.

Stevenson’s blood turned to ice.

He moved quickly, weaving through the crowd.

But when he reached the spot—

Rubert was gone.

That night, back at the safe house, no one spoke much.

Anderson sat on the floor with a glass of scotch. Clara paced. Stevenson stared at the empty fireplace.

Finally, Clara said, “What if he’s undercover? Deep cover?”

Stevenson shook his head. “Or what if he’s not the man we thought?”

Anderson looked up. “Then we bring him in. Or we stop him.”

Foxworth’s voice crackled through the radio on the shelf.

“Change of plans,” he said. “We just received word. Rubert is meeting with a contact tomorrow night. Your new mission is to intercept.”

The line went dead.

Chapter 12: The Man in the Shadows

The night air in London was unusually still. No rain. No sirens. Just the quiet hum of war beneath the city's skin.

Inside the safe house, tension hung like damp laundry. Maps were spread across the table. Pins jabbed into key streets and alleys. The radio hissed with static before Foxworth's voice crackled through again.

"Rubert's expected near Lambeth Bridge, 2100 hours. Watch, follow, and record. Do *not* engage unless fired upon. He may still be one of us."

Stevenson turned off the radio. "We'll see about that."

Clara zipped up her coat. Her lips were set in a line of steel. "He saved us. Don't forget that."

Anderson grabbed his pistol and tucked it into his waistband. "Yeah. And now he might be the reason more of us die. Let's hope it's just a misunderstanding and not a betrayal. I hate tragic endings."

At 2045, they split into positions near the bridge. Fog rolled off the Thames, blanketing the lamps and soaking into every crack of London's bones.

Stevenson crouched on the rooftop of an abandoned textile shop, binoculars steady.

Anderson loitered as a vagrant near a fruit cart, feeding pigeons with breadcrumbs from his pocket.

Clara sat inside a black taxi parked along the curb, engine idling, lipstick flawless, a camera rigged to her handbag.

Then, at 2103, he appeared.

Commander Rubert. Wearing a long coat, hat pulled low. No cane. No limp. Just confidence in every step.

He moved with purpose through the mist and stopped beneath the bridge arch.

A second figure emerged from the shadows—taller, thinner, draped in gray. A man with a face no one could see.

Stevenson zoomed in. Couldn't recognize him.

They exchanged a package. Fast. Fluid. Not military standard—civilian code.

Then Rubert leaned in, whispered something, and turned.

He was walking away.

"Should we follow the second guy?" Clara's voice crackled through Stevenson's earpiece.

"No," he whispered. "We follow *Rubert*."

Rubert's trail led them through narrow alleys and across the back of Westminster.

Stevenson followed from the rooftops, Clara from the taxi, Anderson tailing close enough to count footsteps.

Rubert finally stopped at a quiet church.

He entered. Alone.

Anderson waited five seconds, then slipped in after him.

The church was empty—candles burning at the altar, air thick with incense.

"Commander?" Anderson whispered.

From the shadows, Rubert stepped forward.

Alive. Whole. And looking like he'd aged five years in two months.

"I thought it might be you, Sergeant," Rubert said, voice steady.

Anderson didn't raise his gun. "Then you should've expected backup."

Stevenson and Clara entered from the rear door.

Rubert saw them, and something shifted in his face—relief? Regret?

Clara spoke first. "Why? Why are you meeting with the enemy?"

Rubert sighed. "Because I had no choice. Berlin has my sister. They found her in Belgium. They're using her to make me leak misinformation. But I've twisted it—fed them only false data."

Stevenson stepped forward. "You expect us to believe that?"

"I've left a trail," Rubert said. "Foxworth knows. Or he will. I left him proof this morning. Documents, recordings, copies of my contacts. I've kept you all out of it."

Anderson narrowed his eyes. "Then why disappear? Why *pretend* to be dead?"

Rubert looked down. "Because I didn't want you following me. If they knew you were close, they'd use you too."

The church doors burst open.

Foxworth entered, flanked by agents in trench coats.

"We got your message," he said to Rubert. "And your proof. Just came through two hours ago. You've bought yourself one hell of a mess... but maybe you just saved half the damn front."

Rubert nodded, eyes closed in relief.

And then—

A shot.

One of Foxworth's men collapsed.

Gunfire erupted from the choir loft.

"Ambush!" Foxworth yelled, diving for cover.

Clara pulled Stevenson down behind a pew.

Anderson fired upward. "There were *two* of them at the bridge!"

The traitor—whoever he was—had followed Rubert, waited, and now unleashed chaos to silence him.

Rubert crawled to the altar, grabbing a sidearm from his coat. "I'll draw him out!"

"No!" Stevenson shouted.

But Rubert had already moved.

He fired upward—two quick shots—and the figure above crumpled, crashing down onto the pews.

Dead. Masked.

Foxworth approached the body and ripped the mask off.

Everyone froze.

It was **Colonel Henrik Vale**, from Allied logistics. One of the six on the list. He'd been Clara's superior for two months.

Black Hyena.

Back at the safe house, it was quiet.

Foxworth cleaned his glasses, pacing.

"Rubert's name is clear. The recordings he left confirmed it—he's been playing triple agent, balancing on a razor's edge."

Anderson poured coffee for everyone. "So who's the new bad guy?"

Foxworth nodded toward Vale's body—now zipped and tagged.

"Colonel Vale. Cunning. Clean. Always passed messages through hidden ciphers in requisition forms. He almost shifted an entire battalion into a trap."

Stevenson looked at Rubert. "You didn't just save yourself. You saved all of us."

Rubert sat heavily in a chair. "Doesn't feel like a win."

Clara offered him a mug. "It is one. A messy one. But a win."

Anderson raised his cup. "To the man who came back from the dead."

Rubert chuckled. "Let's hope I don't have to do it again."

That night, Clara and Stevenson stood on the rooftop.

London below was quiet again.

"Did you ever think this war would be about masks?" she asked.

He shook his head. "I thought it'd be bullets and tanks. Turns out, it's lies and loyalties."

She leaned against him. "At least we know who we are."

He wrapped an arm around her. "Yeah. We do."

From the street, Anderson's voice floated up.

"Oi! I found a place selling actual butter. Come down before I eat it with a spoon!"

Clara laughed. "You'd better go. He's dangerous when hungry."

Chapter 13: Desert Whispers and Cairo Lies

The sand was a living thing.

It shifted, sighed, scraped at boots, and clung to skin like forgotten sins. Cairo, blistering and blinding, was a world away from London's fog and damp cellars—but Stevenson, Anderson, Clara, and Rubert had been sent here not for the weather, but for secrets buried beneath the dunes.

The war had moved. Or perhaps, *followed* them.

And behind it, the shadow of something older than gunpowder or tanks—a trail of betrayal that stretched across continents, whispered through ancient tombs, and now pointed toward one enigmatic name:

Project Caldera.

It began with a summons.

Foxworth had flown in via Gibraltar, looking sunburnt and sleep-starved.

"There's something brewing out here," he said, dragging a finger across a battered map of Egypt. "The Nazis have been excavating ruins—not just for treasure or propaganda. They're looking for...something specific."

Anderson leaned in. "Mummies with machine guns?"

Clara elbowed him. "Not now."

Foxworth continued. "We've intercepted telegrams—coded with the old *Vatican cipher*. They mention coordinates in the Valley of the Kings. Phrases like 'the gateway beneath,' and one name repeated: **Helena Bauer**."

Rubert stiffened. “She’s not just an archaeologist. She used to work for British Intelligence.”

“And defected,” Foxworth added. “1940. Disappeared. Rumor has it she joined a German division that dabbles in ‘alternative warfare’—a mix of science, history, and lunacy.”

Stevenson frowned. “You think she’s leading a Nazi dig?”

“Worse,” said Foxworth. “I think she’s running the whole damn operation.”

They arrived in Luxor posing as British museum officials. Their guide, a wiry local named Farouk, spoke five languages and had a sixth reserved for swearing.

“Too many men go into desert,” he said, shaking his head. “Too few come out.”

Clara asked, “Do the Germans have many soldiers near the valley?”

Farouk nodded. “Tents. Trucks. Digging. But...strange. They don’t dig in *obvious* places. They dig in rock, not tomb. Like they’re looking for door.”

Stevenson didn’t like the sound of that.

The next morning, the team surveyed the site from a bluff. Below, German engineers and archaeologists buzzed around scaffolding and generators. At the center, a large sandstone wall, marked with recent chiselings and strange symbols—ancient Egyptian with Greek script overlays.

Clara snapped photos. “Those aren’t decorative glyphs. They’re coordinates.”

“Coordinates to what?” Rubert asked.

Anderson squinted. “That’s the question, isn’t it?”

They decided to infiltrate that night.

Disguised in stolen Afrika Korps uniforms and posing as a delivery crew, they maneuvered past the guards and into the camp. Anderson improvised a story about “missing radio tubes,” which inexplicably worked.

Inside the central tent, Stevenson found crates of strange equipment—oscilloscopes, electromagnetic scanners, and one thick leather-bound notebook marked **Caldera**.

Clara flipped through it. Her brow furrowed.

“This isn’t just archaeology. They’re testing for *sound waves*—under the sand. Looking for hollow spaces. And this—” she pointed to a page “—mentions seismic resonance and something called the ‘Axis Well.’”

Rubert picked up a coded telegram: “Helena Bauer arriving tomorrow.”

“We need to intercept her,” Stevenson said. “If she’s leading this, we end it now.”

Anderson opened a crate. “Or we blow it up now.”

Stevenson hesitated. “No. Let’s see what she’s really after.”

Helena arrived the next afternoon by truck convoy—tall, pale, and dressed like Lawrence of Arabia’s twin sister. Her hair was pinned tightly, her sunglasses mirrored. She looked around the dig like a queen returning to her throne.

Rubert watched from behind a rock ridge. “She hasn’t changed.”

“You knew her?” Clara asked.

“Once,” he said. “Brilliant. Ruthless. And charming as hell.”

Anderson chewed his lip. “So... basically your ex?”

Rubert didn’t answer.

That night, they trailed Helena to the dig’s heart.

She stepped to the sandstone wall, whispered something in German—and pressed her hand against a carved panel.

It *moved.*

A narrow seam of stone slid inward with a low rumble. Sand poured down like an hourglass breaking.

A tunnel had been opened.

Helena entered.

“We’re going in,” Stevenson whispered.

Rubert nodded. “No lights. No guns unless absolutely needed.”

Anderson muttered, “Great. Trapped in a Nazi tomb with a woman obsessed with ancient doom. Just like Christmas at my uncle’s.”

Inside, the tunnel sloped downward, growing colder with every step. Faint torchlight flickered from sconces, recently lit. The walls were covered with more symbols—none of them Egyptian.

Greek. Latin. Hebrew. Even Sanskrit.

“What is this place?” Clara whispered.

“A collection of ancient warnings,” Rubert replied.

At the bottom, they found Helena in a large chamber. She stood before a stone disc set into the floor, surrounded by bronze rods and cables hooked to a generator.

She hadn't heard them.

Clara began filming. Rubert stepped forward.

"Helena."

She turned slowly. Her face didn't show surprise—just calculation.

"James," she said softly. "I was wondering when you'd find me."

Stevenson raised his pistol. "Step away from the disc."

Helena smiled. "Still the soldier. But this isn't a weapon. It's *older* than any war."

Anderson stepped behind her. "What does it *do*?"

She gestured at the disc. "Legend says the Caldera was a gate—built by a civilization before Egypt. Before history. They believed sound could bend space. And this—" she touched the disc gently "—is the last of its kind."

Rubert stepped forward. "You'd hand this to *Hitler*?"

Her eyes burned. "No. I'd *replace* him. The world needs power. But the right kind."

Stevenson narrowed his eyes. "You're insane."

Helena sighed. "That's disappointing. I wanted you on my side, Stevenson."

Then she pressed the disc.

A low hum filled the room—like a choir underwater.

The floor began to vibrate.

Cracks split the walls. The disc glowed.

"Get out!" Clara screamed.

They ran.

Behind them, the chamber collapsed—sand, rock, stone crashing like thunder.

Helena did not follow.

Outside, the camp was in chaos. German guards scrambled. Tents collapsed.

Stevenson dragged Clara behind a truck. Rubert held up a detonator.

Anderson nodded. "Do it."

Boom.

The dig site exploded—dust, flame, and screams rising into the Egyptian night.

Back in Cairo, the report was simple:

Operation Caldera Terminated. Target lost. Tunnel destroyed. Nazi project dismantled.

But Rubert knew better.

"She wanted us to see it," he said quietly. "She knew we'd follow. She knew we'd *stop* her. This was only the beginning."

Stevenson stared at the desert horizon. "Then we find where the trail leads next."

Anderson slumped into a chair. “Unless it’s Antarctica. Then I vote we let someone else handle it.”

Chapter 14: Shadows on the Mediterranean

The *Höllenhai* was a beast of steel and salt.

One of the Kriegsmarine's finest heavy cruisers, it cut through the Mediterranean like a shark in silk. Bristling with anti-aircraft turrets, radar dishes, and a belly full of torpedoes, the ship was en route to Athens. But this wasn't a routine supply run. Hidden in its armored hold was a crate marked **CALDERA-A3**—sealed, encoded, and protected by some of the Reich's deadliest men.

Inside that crate was something Helena Bauer had died—or disappeared—for.

And Stevenson's team had orders to get it back.

Foxworth's voice was flat as a knife as he briefed them in a makeshift command center in Malta.

"We intercepted intel from one of Helena's abandoned radios. There's a third device from the Caldera chamber. Apparently, she smuggled it out before the collapse. The Nazis loaded it onto the *Höllenhai* in Tripoli. It's heading for a secret lab near Mount Olympus."

Clara raised an eyebrow. "Myths on top of myths."

Anderson looked interested. "What's in the crate? A glowing orb? Map to Atlantis? Hitler's favorite waffle recipe?"

Foxworth didn't smile. "We don't know. But if Bauer wanted it saved, you can bet it's not just some museum piece."

They needed a ship.

They found one—barely seaworthy, rusted, and captained by an ex-fisherman turned smuggler named Dimitri, who looked like Poseidon's more hungover cousin.

"It float. It move. It doesn't smell like goat anymore," Dimitri grinned, slapping the side of his trawler, *Elena's Gift.*

Anderson muttered, "Confidence-inspiring."

Still, under the cover of darkness, they departed Malta, headed into open waters with nothing but a compass, a map of German naval routes, and a stolen Enigma codebook Clara had charmed off a former contact in Alexandria.

Two days later, at dusk, they spotted her.

The *Höllenhai* loomed on the horizon, a silent fortress.

Rubert, peering through binoculars, said grimly, "We're not taking that ship by force."

Stevenson nodded. "We sneak in. Steal the crate. Get out before they notice."

Anderson strapped on his diving gear. "So just a casual break-in aboard a Nazi warship. Wonderful. Remind me to retire somewhere *boring* after this."

They approached at midnight, using the shadows of a passing cargo vessel as cover. Anderson and Stevenson dove in, swimming silently to the hull of the *Höllenhai* while Clara and Rubert remained on the trawler, monitoring communications.

The climb was brutal.

Salt stung their eyes. Steel scraped their palms. But they made it to the loading bay, timing their entrance between rotating searchlights.

Inside, the smell was oil, sweat, and cordite.

Stevenson motioned. “Cargo hold. This way.”

Anderson led, ducking past two guards with a silent knockout maneuver that involved a wrench, a sneeze, and what might have been a dance move.

Down in the hold, they found it.

The crate sat at the far end, guarded by a lone officer reading a dog-eared issue of *Signal* magazine.

Stevenson whispered, “Distract him.”

Anderson grinned.

He tiptoed to a stack of crates, knocked one over with a loud *bang*, and yelled in a thick Russian accent, “Comrade pigeon! You escape again!”

The guard blinked. “What the—”

Too late. Stevenson knocked him out cold.

Anderson winced. “Comrade pigeon? Really?”

“Worked, didn’t it?”

They pried open the crate.

Inside was... a sphere.

About the size of a basketball. Made of dark metal with faint carvings etched into its surface. It pulsed faintly, like a heartbeat.

Stevenson whispered, “Is it... alive?”

Anderson didn’t answer.

Because the sphere *hummed.*

And every light in the cargo bay flickered.

Then the alarm sounded.

"All hands to stations! Intruders on board!"

The ship roared to life.

Stevenson and Anderson ran for the port side, carrying the crate. Searchlights swept across the deck.

From the *Elena's Gift*, Rubert shouted through the radio, "Jump now!"

They did.

The water exploded around them as German soldiers opened fire.

Rubert and Clara tossed ropes and pulled them in as the trawler roared away, dodging tracer rounds.

Anderson gasped as he lay on the deck, soaked. "Well... that went exactly how I expected."

Clara examined the sphere. "It's not radioactive. But it's... reacting to proximity."

Rubert nodded. "We'll take it to the Athens safe house. Figure out what it's meant to do."

Foxworth radioed in as they neared the coast. "Good work. But you're not safe yet. We just decoded another message. Someone from Helena's old circle is already in Greece. Looking for you."

That night in Athens, the sphere began to glow brighter.

Clara stared at it. "I think it's guiding us."

And on its surface, a symbol began to form.

A mountain.

And beneath it, a word.

ARGYROS.

Chapter 15: The Monastery of Argyros

The mountain watched them as they approached.

Mount Argyros wasn't the tallest peak in Greece, nor the most famous—but it loomed like an old man's secret, grey and hunched, its summit lost in low-hanging clouds. At its foot stood the monastery, weathered by time and war, surrounded by olive trees and silence.

Stevenson adjusted the strap on the crate as they climbed the narrow mountain path. The Caldera sphere, now hidden in a canvas bag, pulsed faintly against his back. Every few steps, it gave off a low hum—like a tuning fork resonating in his spine.

Anderson walked beside him, panting. "Why... do secret Nazi artifacts... always end up in mountains?"

Clara replied, climbing ahead of them, "Because deserts and mountaintops are the only places left the rest of us don't check."

Rubert, who hadn't broken a sweat, said nothing.

He knew this place.

They reached the monastery gates by late morning. Massive wooden doors carved with saints and serpents greeted them.

A monk opened the gate.

He was small, ancient, and looked like he'd once arm-wrestled time itself—and lost. "Yes?"

Rubert stepped forward. "We need to see Father Matthaios. Tell him Rubert has come."

The monk's eyes widened. He nodded and disappeared into the shadows.

Anderson muttered, “Old friends?”

Rubert didn’t answer.

The monastery smelled of wax, old stone, and incense. It was quiet—unnaturally so.

Father Matthaios met them in the courtyard. Tall and severe, with a beard like a prophet and eyes like knives, he greeted Rubert with a long look.

“You swore you’d never come back.”

Rubert replied, “And you swore you’d stay out of politics.”

The priest exhaled sharply. “War has no borders anymore. Nor faith.”

Clara gently stepped between them. “We’re looking for answers. The object we carry—”

“—Is not meant for man,” Matthaios interrupted, eyes fixed on the crate.

“We don’t want to use it,” Stevenson said. “We want to *stop* the ones who do.”

That night, under the chapel’s candlelight, Matthaios led them to a hidden chamber beneath the altar.

The catacombs were carved into the rock, older than the monastery itself. Byzantine mosaics covered the walls—scenes of angels, floods, wars, and stars falling from the sky.

But one wall stood out: it depicted a sphere—just like the one they carried—held by a faceless figure with open hands. Beneath it, an inscription in Greek:

“To awaken the sphere is to call the eye. To silence it is to save the world.”

Clara translated softly. “The Eye?”

Matthaios nodded. “It’s not a weapon in itself. It’s a *key*. One of three. They must never be brought together.”

Rubert asked, “So Helena didn’t find just relics—she found *instructions*.”

Stevenson said, “And now someone else is following them.”

At midnight, they placed the sphere on a stone pedestal.

It began to glow brighter.

Suddenly, a shadow moved across the chamber wall.

Gunshots.

The candles blew out.

Chaos erupted.

Stevenson tackled Clara to the ground as bullets pinged off stone.

Anderson rolled into cover and returned fire, dropping one assailant.

“Who the hell are these guys?” he shouted.

Rubert growled, “Not Nazis. Mercenaries. Hired hands.”

“By who?”

A voice echoed from the darkness. “By the one who wants what Helena couldn’t have.”

Footsteps emerged.

A man in a dark overcoat and gloves stepped into the flickering light—tall, grey-haired, with eyes that glinted like ice.

Clara gasped. “General Karl Neumann.”

Rubert stiffened. “Dead since ‘43. Or so we thought.”

Neumann smiled thinly. “Rumors of my death were... experimental.”

He gestured to the sphere. “Give me the key.”

Stevenson raised his pistol. “Not a chance.”

Neumann nodded. “Then let’s make this unpleasant.”

He snapped his fingers.

More mercenaries descended.

Anderson growled, “You know, for a secret chamber full of ancient warnings, this place gets *real* crowded.”

In the chaos, Father Matthaios was shot. As he collapsed, he pressed a small stone into Rubert’s hand.

“The seal... Mount Elikonas...”

Rubert caught him as he died. “No. Not now.”

Stevenson fired a final shot and yelled, “Fall back!”

They escaped through the catacombs, fire and footsteps chasing them through the dark.

Behind them, Neumann secured the sphere.

His eyes gleamed as it began to *sing*.

Back in their trawler off the coast, battered and bloodied, the team regrouped.

Clara whispered, “He has it now.”

Stevenson stared into the horizon. “Then we get it back. No matter where it leads.”

Rubert uncurled his hand.

Inside, the stone from Matthaios bore a symbol:

A seal.

And coordinates carved in Latin.

Anderson leaned in.

“Next stop?”

Rubert answered:

“Mount Elikonas.”

Chapter 16: The Echoes of Elikonas

The road to Mount Elikonas was carved in shadows.

Nestled in the heart of Greece, the mountain stood like a quiet sentinel, tall and jagged, covered in whispering pine forests and pockets of white mist. Unlike the touristy peaks of Olympus or Parnassus, Elikonas was mostly untouched. Locals said it was cursed. That people who ventured too far heard voices in the fog—and sometimes didn't come back at all.

Perfect place for a Nazi resurrection plot, Stevenson thought grimly.

They traveled in a rickety army truck stolen from a German depot, bouncing along half-finished mountain roads. The silence inside was thick, broken only by the rumble of the tires and Anderson's occasional hummed rendition of a swing tune.

"So let me get this straight," he finally said, munching an olive. "We lost the shiny doom-sphere to a supposedly dead Nazi general with cheekbones carved by ice, and now we're chasing ancient monk riddles up a haunted mountain because a dying priest handed Rubert a rock."

Rubert didn't respond.

Clara did. "Yes, Anderson. That's exactly what happened."

Anderson nodded. "Just checking we're still grounded in reality."

They reached a ruined monastery near the summit at dusk. It was barely a skeleton—crumbling archways, moss-eaten pillars, and a chapel roof collapsed long ago. According to Matthaios' stone, this was where the "Seal of the Eye" lay hidden.

"Split up," Rubert said. "Clara and I will check the archives. You two take the chapel ruins."

Stevenson and Anderson wandered among the fallen stones, their boots crunching broken tiles and dry leaves.

"I hate how quiet it is," Anderson murmured. "No birds. No bugs. Even the mountain's holding its breath."

Stevenson knelt beside a sunken floor mosaic. "Look at this."

It was a circular design—similar to the markings on the sphere. At the center was a triangle surrounded by concentric rings, with Greek inscriptions spiraling outward.

Anderson traced it with his fingers. "This the seal?"

"Could be."

Then, they heard it.

A low, *vibrating* hum—like a sound their ears didn't catch but their bones did.

The mosaic began to pulse faintly.

Meanwhile, Clara and Rubert entered what was left of the monastery's scriptorium. Scrolls and parchment had long turned to dust, but Clara found a few carved tablets sealed in clay.

She carefully broke one open—and found a map.

Or rather, a layered diagram.

"Three keys. Three vaults. But only one gate," she whispered.

Rubert leaned over her shoulder. "So the Caldera sphere was one of the keys. What are the other two?"

Clara's eyes narrowed. "Not objects. People."

Back at the mosaic, the humming grew stronger.

Suddenly, Anderson stumbled.

“Stevenson—do you see that?”

The ground beneath the design rippled like water. Then the center *cracked open*, revealing a circular staircase plunging into the dark.

“Why is it always stairs?” Anderson grumbled.

They descended carefully, lantern in hand.

The air was colder underground. Damp. Heavy with age.

At the bottom, they found a chamber lit by strange blue torches—cold flame that didn’t burn.

In the center was a stone pedestal, and atop it... a second sphere.

But this one was different.

Smaller. Darker. Covered in veins of obsidian that pulsed like a heartbeat.

Stevenson stepped forward. “Is this the second key?”

Before Anderson could answer, a voice echoed from the darkness:

“No. That is the *lock*.”

Neumann.

He emerged from the shadows flanked by two mercenaries. He held the original Caldera sphere in one hand, glowing bright as a star.

“You brought me to the gate,” he said. “How kind.”

Stevenson raised his gun. “Drop it.”

Neumann chuckled. “You still think this is about war, Sergeant? This goes far beyond Reichs and flags. Helena understood that. In the end.”

Clara and Rubert appeared in the entrance behind Neumann. Clara held a flare gun.

“Step away from the pedestal.”

Neumann turned slightly, unfazed. “The seal doesn’t need all three. Just the right voice.”

He placed the Caldera sphere into a slot in the pedestal.

Everything *shifted.*

The ground trembled.

Rocks fell from the ceiling.

Anderson yelled, “Not another earthquake!”

A circular glyph formed on the floor.

Energy surged upward—a column of white-blue light.

The second sphere began to *sing*.

Not just sound—*memory*.

Visions flashed in each of their minds.

Ancient cities burning. Towers reaching the stars. A machine larger than any temple, forged in a forgotten language. And at the center—an *eye*.

Not a symbol.

An actual, pulsing, sentient eye.

Watching.

Alive.

Neumann gasped. "It's true."

But the eye turned to him—and in that moment, his body convulsed.

His mercenaries screamed.

Anderson yanked Stevenson back. "We have to *close it!*"

Clara rushed to the pedestal, flipping the Caldera sphere out of its socket.

The light stopped.

Neumann collapsed, smoking, his eyes blank.

The second sphere darkened.

Silence returned.

Hours later, they stood above ground again, shaken.

Rubert tossed the second sphere into a satchel. "We can't destroy them. Not yet. But we can keep them apart."

Clara nodded. "There's one more."

Anderson exhaled. “Let me guess. It’s somewhere cold. Remote. And probably crawling with the last of Hitler’s private knitting circle.”

Stevenson turned to Clara. “Where’s the third key?”

She looked at him.

And said one word:

“Iceland.”

Chapter 17: The Fire Beneath Ice

The Icelandic coast was a riddle of ice and silence.

Jagged black rock jutted from the sea like broken teeth, waves smashing against them with eternal force. Cold mist cloaked everything in a shroud of breathless gray. It was the kind of place stories were born—or came to die.

As their aircraft descended toward Reykjavík, Clara looked out the window, gripping a small notebook. Her fingers were pale, tense.

Stevenson noticed. “What’s bothering you?”

She didn’t answer at first. Then: “This wasn’t supposed to be real. Helena was chasing myths. Now we’re following her steps through ancient seals, ghost generals, and sentient relics.”

Anderson leaned in from the next seat. “Don't forget ‘half-dead monks’ and ‘mountains that hum.’ You left those off the brochure.”

Clara almost smiled. “We’re close. The third key is here. But this time... I don’t think we’re alone.”

Iceland’s winter had already begun creeping over the land. With endless daylight fading fast, they had only a few hours of sun each day—and even less time before Neumann’s allies caught up.

According to the cracked coordinates hidden in Matthaios’ stone and cross-checked with Helena’s last known journal entry, the third relic lay buried deep within an old volcanic cave system beneath the Vatnajökull glacier.

Rubert arranged transport.

They would travel across the ice in an old snowcat tracked vehicle—no roads, no landmarks, just satellite directions, fraying nerves, and endless frost.

The journey took two days.

Inside the vehicle, Clara mapped out the glacier's seismic zones while Anderson, bundled like a walking blanket, complained every 10 minutes.

"I can't feel my toes," he said. "Or my personality. I'm one scarf away from becoming a knitted corpse."

Stevenson chuckled. "Don't worry. You'll freeze fashionably."

Rubert interrupted. "We're here."

They stopped at the edge of a jagged ice ridge. Beneath it was a sinkhole—an ancient lava tube partially collapsed, yawning open like a wound in the glacier.

They descended on ropes.

The cave beneath was vast and pitch black.

Their lanterns flickered off shimmering walls of volcanic glass and frozen columns. The air was unnaturally warm near the center—a geothermal vent. They followed the heat.

Then they saw it.

A chamber, half-buried in ice and rock.

Built from stone that didn't match the surrounding geology. Old. Smooth. And inscribed with glyphs identical to the ones they'd seen under Elikonas.

This was it.

The final vault.

Inside, they found the third sphere.

It sat atop a pedestal carved from obsidian, surrounded by skeletal remains—monks, maybe. Or guards. It was smaller than the other two, and it emitted no hum.

It was *silent.*

Anderson didn't trust it. "Too quiet. Even the spooky ones glow or sing."

Clara stepped forward slowly. "This one's dormant. The Eye can't reach here. Not yet."

Rubert examined the pedestal. "There's an inscription."

He read it aloud:

"Only when the three stand united shall the world awaken. But not all awakenings are rebirth."

Stevenson looked around. "So the legend was real. But the warning is clearer now. The keys don't open something new—they *resurrect* something old."

Anderson muttered, "What could be worse than that?"

The answer came quickly.

A sound from above.

Snow shifting.

Voices.

They weren't alone.

Explosions ripped through the cave entrance. Ice rained down as figures in black rappelled into the vault—mercenaries in updated SS gear, moving with precision.

Leading them was a woman with silver-blonde hair and a scar down her left cheek.

Clara's breath caught. "Ilsa?"

The woman smirked. "Hello, sister."

In the confusion, Stevenson grabbed the third sphere, tucking it into his satchel.

Bullets ricocheted off stone as Rubert returned fire.

Ilsa's troops were fast—but Rubert's team was faster.

Anderson lobbed a flare toward a natural steam vent—it ignited with a deafening *BOOM*, collapsing one side of the cave and buying them precious seconds.

They scrambled toward a narrow exit route Clara had mapped.

Ilsa's voice echoed behind them. "You can't run forever! The Eye has seen you!"

They emerged from the cave into the freezing dawn, lungs burning.

As they loaded back into the snowcat, Stevenson looked at Clara. "Sister?"

Clara exhaled shakily. "We were both recruited by Helena. Ilsa believed in using the relics as weapons. I left. She didn't."

Anderson clutched the steering wheel. “And now she’s trying to wake up something ancient and murderous, just to prove a point?”

Rubert handed him a map. “Then we stop her.”

Clara’s fingers brushed the three spheres. They vibrated faintly—*together*.

“The Eye is aware of us now,” she said softly. “And it’s beginning to remember.”

Chapter 18: The Eye Awakens

Somewhere off the coast of Malta, far beneath the surface of the Mediterranean Sea, a forgotten temple lay buried under coral and centuries of silence.

It was here the final phase would begin.

Back in a nondescript safehouse on the outskirts of Athens, Rubert laid the three spheres across a wide stone table. The spheres pulsed faintly, each vibrating at a different rhythm—almost like a heartbeat out of sync. Together, they were beginning to hum a language none of them could understand, but all could feel.

Clara hovered nearby, pale but calm. Her voice was barely above a whisper. "This... this is what Helena feared."

Anderson peeked from behind a cup of thick Greek coffee. "We've now got three cosmic marbles that sing to each other. What happens if someone actually *unites* them?"

Stevenson looked across at Rubert. “You’ve studied Helena’s notes more than any of us. What did she believe the Eye really was?”

Rubert didn’t answer immediately. He looked tired. Older than he had before.

“She didn’t know,” he said finally. “She only guessed. She believed the Eye wasn’t a weapon. Not in the traditional sense. It was something ancient... watching. Waiting. A memory left behind by a civilization far older than ours.”

Anderson scoffed. “Aliens?”

“No,” Clara said. “Not aliens. Us. Before us. A cycle that resets every few thousand years. Helena believed the Eye was a warning left behind after the last fall.”

Stevenson rubbed his temples. “Then why would anyone *want* to activate it?”

Rubert met his eyes. “Because some people think they can *control* it.”

The safehouse’s encrypted radio cracked to life.

An urgent signal—intercepted from Ilsa’s forces.

Clara translated. “They’re on the move. Setting sail for an undersea site... coordinates off the coast of Gozo.”

Rubert’s face went hard. “The Temple of Hades.”

Anderson blinked. “I’m sorry, *what?*”

“It’s older than written history,” Rubert said. “A megalithic site now submerged. It was rumored to be one of three gates to the underworld. But Helena found evidence it was a place of storage—not death. A tomb. A vault for something that should not awaken.”

Stevenson tightened his gloves. “Then we’re going underwater.”

Their team chartered a research submersible using forged documents and stolen UN funding codes. The vessel was called *The Nereid*, a deep-sea exploration ship retrofitted for cold-water descent.

As they sailed through stormy waters, the sea grew darker, angrier.

Anderson stared at the roiling waves and muttered, “This is how I die. Drowned, cold, and annoyed.”

Clara smirked. “We’ll all be cold.”

The descent into the abyss was slow and silent.

The three spheres sat in a padded crate between Stevenson and Clara, their glow now steady and synchronized.

As the Nereid passed 700 feet, the ocean became ink.

Then the sonar pinged.

A structure.

Large. Circular. Covered in coral and sediment.

Clara pointed. “That’s it.”

Through the porthole, they could see stone pillars rising from the ocean floor—twisted, carved with strange symbols, half-swallowed by time. A central spire stood at the center like a broken tooth. It was ancient. Alien. And yet... familiar.

Stevenson whispered, “The Temple of Hades.”

They suited up and descended in pressurized diving suits, dragging the crate behind them in a waterproof shell.

It took twenty minutes to reach the temple entrance.

The doorway was marked with symbols from all three previous vaults—mosaics, glyphs, warnings.

But they had no time for caution.

Ilsa's forces had beaten them there.

Flashes of light burst through the murk.

Gunfire underwater was muffled but deadly.

Rubert signaled to split up.

Stevenson and Anderson flanked right, taking cover behind ruined columns. Rubert and Clara moved straight into the heart of the temple.

In the central chamber, Ilsa stood on a platform with three glowing sockets.

Behind her, a machine of impossible design had begun to stir—half-metal, half-stone, and taller than any cathedral.

Clara stared in disbelief. "It's not just a vault... it's the Eye itself."

Ilsa turned slowly. Her silver hair floated like a halo in the water.

"You came too late," she said through her voice comm. "It's already begun."

She dropped the first two spheres into the sockets.

The temple *shuddered*.

Light pulsed from every wall.

Anderson shouted, “Third one’s in the crate—she doesn’t have it!”

Ilsa smiled. “Then give it to me, or you’ll drown here with your principles.”

Stevenson stepped forward, holding the last sphere.

“You don’t understand what you’re doing.”

Ilsa laughed. “I understand perfectly. This world is weak. Broken. The Eye will cleanse it.”

Stevenson held the sphere just out of reach. “And you think it’ll spare you?”

“I *know* it will. I’ve seen it. In dreams. In echoes.”

Clara moved silently, unnoticed, to the side of the machine.

She placed a small device—a compact explosive—into a maintenance hatch.

Anderson covered her with a harpoon launcher. “Just say the word.”

Rubert moved behind Stevenson and whispered, “We can’t stop her if she activates all three. The Eye will wake.”

Stevenson exhaled.

Then threw the sphere to Clara.

Everything happened at once.

Clara caught the sphere and hurled it into the depths—away from the machine.

Ilsa screamed.

Anderson fired.

Rubert tackled one of Ilsa's guards.

Stevenson charged.

The sphere sank into the deep.

The machine *paused*. The two active spheres began to dim. The hum died.

Ilsa, furious, dove after the sinking relic—but Rubert grabbed her mid-dive, locking her in place.

Clara hit the detonator.

BOOM.

The explosion cracked the temple floor.

A jet of bubbles surged upward.

Stone began to collapse.

The Eye groaned.

And closed.

They barely made it back to the sub before the collapse finished.

The temple was buried once more, hidden under rubble and sediment. The third sphere was lost in the depths, unreachable.

Ilsa was gone—swept away by the current or crushed beneath stone.

The Eye… slept.

For now.

Back on the Nereid, soaked and exhausted, the four of them sat in silence.

Anderson finally broke it. “Next time, can we stop an evil plot in a nice dry library?”

Clara smiled weakly. “You’d complain about the lighting.”

Rubert looked at the two remaining spheres. “We hide these. Separate them. Forever.”

Stevenson nodded. “And pray no one ever finds the third.”

Somewhere, far beneath the ocean, the third sphere settled into darkness.

It pulsed—once.

Twice.

And then went still.

Chapter 19: The Ghost That Watched

Six weeks later.

The frost-bitten chaos of Iceland, the ancient ruins of Greece, and the drowned temple under the Mediterranean felt like a bad dream. Dusty, surreal, and slightly ridiculous if you said it aloud.

Yet here they were—alive.

Mostly.

The team had split up.

Rubert returned to the intelligence community's shadows—too valuable and too dangerous to stay above ground. Clara had been quietly absorbed into an international archaeological think tank with deep funding and even deeper secrets.

Anderson?

He claimed he was writing a novel about the whole thing. "It'll be part memoir, part thriller, and part food blog. Chapter One: How Not to Die in a Submarine."

Stevenson had taken the longest to settle. His military record had been patched clean, his heroics buried under redacted files. All he'd kept was the notebook Clara gave him.

And a photograph.

The last one they took together—him, Anderson, Clara, and Rubert, standing in front of the Nereid. Rubert even smiled a little. Sort of.

It was late evening in Verona, Italy. Stevenson now lived there under the name “Mark Dante,” which he thought sounded mysterious but mostly just confused the locals.

He ran a garage. Fixed cars. Tuned engines. Drank espresso. Told tourists that “no, Juliet’s balcony isn’t actually hers.”

And once a week, he visited the lakeside.

Not for reflection.

But because he wasn’t sure if he was still being watched.

The spheres had been split and hidden across three continents.

Rubert personally ensured one stayed deep inside the Vatican’s archives, under enough ancient bureaucracy to confuse even the most committed treasure hunter.

Clara entrusted hers to the Bodleian Library—disguised as a forgotten alchemical orb inside an obscure reading room that required six keys and an oath in Latin.

The third… was lost.

But lost doesn’t mean gone.

One quiet Tuesday, as Stevenson was closing up his garage, Anderson strolled in with gelato and two coffees.

“Guess who got offered a job consulting on a film about underwater ruins?” he said cheerfully. “Spoiler: it's me. Apparently, I look like ‘the rogue type’.”

Stevenson smirked. “Let me guess, you’re playing yourself again?”

Anderson winked. “Naturally. Though I demanded a better jawline.”

They sat outside, watching the orange glow fade across the water.

Anderson leaned back. “You think it’s over?”

Stevenson didn’t answer right away. He looked up at the sky, stars barely visible beyond the city glow.

“I think the Eye closed. Not because we won. But because it chose to.”

Anderson frowned. “Creepy.”

“Yeah,” Stevenson said. “But it’s asleep. That’s enough.”

A long silence.

Then Anderson nodded at the back of the garage. “You still got it, don’t you?”

Stevenson didn’t look. “What?”

“The map Clara gave you. The one with the other sites she *didn’t* tell us about.”

This time, Stevenson looked at him.

“I burned it.”

Anderson raised an eyebrow.

“You *burned* it?”

Stevenson stood up, took his keys, and smiled faintly. “No. But I really wanted to.”

Across the world, in a dimly lit room buried beneath Tokyo's neon streets, a hand reached into a steel container.

A hand wearing a familiar ring.

Inside the box sat a broken piece of obsidian.

It pulsed—once.

Softly.

Patiently.

Chapter 20: The Long Sleep

Rain soaked the streets of Tokyo, bouncing off neon signs like static. Under a ramen stall's awning, Clara stirred her noodles thoughtfully.

Across the table sat a woman with red glasses and an expression like she was born suspicious.

Clara leaned in.

"You're sure it was in the container?"

The woman nodded. "My contact said the fragment was found by deep-sea salvagers. Pressure damage. It still pulsed."

Clara's stomach turned. "That shouldn't be possible."

Meanwhile, in Verona, Stevenson was fixing a Vespa when his phone—one that hadn't rung in weeks—buzzed with a single word.

"Tokyo."

He wiped his hands, sighed, and didn't hesitate.

Three Days Later – Tokyo

The gang was back together.

Sort of.

Clara had summoned them with urgency.

Rubert arrived looking sharper than ever, though older somehow. His limp was more noticeable now, but his eyes were still the same—cold steel wrapped in respect.

Anderson came in Hawaiian print and sunglasses.

"I missed you weirdos," he said. "And yes, I brought snacks."

They gathered in a small, secure office under the Japanese Science & History Ministry. On the table sat the object: a shard of the third sphere.

It pulsed—quiet, soft, and undeniably alive.

Stevenson stared at it for a long time.

"We threw it into the trench. It should've been crushed."

Clara nodded grimly. "It didn't need the temple. Or the chamber. Or even all three pieces. It just needed time."

Rubert tapped the edge of the metal table. "It's rebuilding. Regrowing. Like a fungus."

Anderson winced. "So... the Eye's not asleep. It's *healing*."

They began combing through Helena's last journals, the ones Clara never shared until now. Within the pages were sketches, maps, and one page in particular—highlighted in crimson ink:

"The Eye isn't a weapon. It's a memory that wants to be whole. Every time it's found, it whispers its story into the world's bones. If we listen long enough, we forget it's not ours."

Rubert closed the journal slowly.

"It doesn't want to destroy us. It wants us to become it."

That night, Clara made a decision.

"The fragment can't be hidden. Not this time. It has to be erased."

Anderson squinted. "You mean like, delete it? Toss it into a volcano?"

"No," she said. "We bury it in a memory stronger than its own. A counter-story."

The plan was insane.

Beautifully insane.

They would return the shard to where it all began: beneath Mount Elikonas.

There, they would use the ancient fail-safes Helena had identified—a trio of harmonic points designed not to awaken the Eye, but to silence it.

The catch? They had to *synchronize* the relic with its own opposite frequency.

They would essentially overwrite the Eye's memory.

Wipe it clean.

Or die trying.

Mount Elikonas – One Week Later

The cave looked different now.

Quieter. Older.

They hiked in together, the wind screaming above, the fog thick as wool. The air inside the chamber still smelled of dust and time.

Clara placed the shard on the stone dais.

Stevenson adjusted the array of equipment—part scientific, part mystical, mostly improvised.

Anderson stood by with a detonator labeled "Plan B."

Rubert activated the harmonic field.

The shard began to pulse violently.

Then—

The cavern shook.

The floor cracked.

And something *spoke*.

Not in words. Not in sound.

It was a feeling.

An ache in the teeth. A name they'd forgotten they once knew.

Clara stepped forward and pressed her hand to the shard.

She whispered, “Sleep.”

The ground heaved.

And the shard—

Shattered.

Silence.

Then the glow faded.

The tremors stopped.

The cavern exhaled, as though relieved.

They stood still for several minutes, just breathing.

Rubert finally said, “It’s over.”

And for once, no one argued.

Three Months Later – Somewhere Peaceful

Anderson published his “novel.” It sold terribly, but he insisted the critics “just didn’t understand the underwater cult bits.”

Clara returned to her lectures, teaching history the world would never truly know.

Rubert vanished again—some say to Siberia. Others say Argentina.

Stevenson?

He went home.

For real this time.

Back in Verona, he bought a tiny vineyard, planted tomatoes, and finally fixed the bell on the bakery door next door.

Sometimes he'd wake up in the middle of the night expecting the Eye to be there.

Watching.

But it wasn't.

It was gone.

Or... perhaps just dreaming.

But for now, the world was safe.

And quiet.

And free.

Epilogue

A single monk swept the temple floors in northern Greece.

He paused, leaned on his broom, and looked at the stars.

Under the floor, in a box no bigger than a shoebox, something slept.

It pulsed—so faintly, it could've been mistaken for nothing.

But it wasn't.

It waited.

As it always had.

www.ingramcontent.com/pod-product-compliance
Ingram Content Group UK Ltd.
Pitfield, Milton Keynes, MK11 3LW, UK
UKHW030740230726
13954UKWH00020B/135

9 789334 357943